First World War
and Army of Occupation
War Diary
France, Belgium and Germany

16 DIVISION
48 Infantry Brigade,
Brigade Machine Gun Company
24 April 1916 - 28 February 1918

WO95/1975/8

The Naval & Military Press Ltd
www.nmarchive.com
Published in association with The National Archives

Published by

The Naval & Military Press Ltd

Unit 10 Ridgewood Industrial Park,

Uckfield, East Sussex,

TN22 5QE England

Tel: +44 (0) 1825 749494

www.naval-military-press.com

www.nmarchive.com

This diary has been reprinted in facsimile from the original. Any imperfections are inevitably reproduced and the quality may fall short of modern type and cartographic standards.

© Crown Copyright
Images reproduced by permission of The National Archives, London, England, 2015.

Contents

Document type	Place/Title	Date From	Date To
Heading	1975/8 Brigade Machine Gun Company Apr 1916-Feb 1918		
Heading	16th Division 48th Infy Bde 48th Machine Gun Coy. Apl 1916-Feb 1918		
War Diary	Grantham	24/04/1916	25/04/1916
War Diary	Havre	26/04/1916	27/04/1916
War Diary	Noeux-Les-Mines	28/04/1916	28/04/1916
War Diary	Houchin	29/04/1916	29/04/1916
War Diary	Trenches Hulluch Sector	30/04/1916	30/04/1916
War Diary	Philosophe	30/04/1916	30/04/1916
War Diary	Trenches Hulluch Section	01/05/1916	02/05/1916
War Diary	Noeux-Les Mines	03/05/1916	05/05/1916
War Diary	Trenches Hulluch Section	06/05/1916	15/05/1916
War Diary	Trenches Bis 14 Section	16/05/1916	24/05/1916
War Diary	Noeux-Les-Mines	25/05/1916	27/05/1916
War Diary	Trenches 14 Bis Section	28/05/1916	31/05/1916
War Diary	Trenches Loos Section	31/05/1916	31/05/1916
War Diary	Trenches 14 Bis Section & Loss Section	01/06/1916	01/06/1916
War Diary	Trenches Loos Section	02/06/1916	02/06/1916
War Diary	Trenches & Loss Section	03/06/1916	03/06/1916
War Diary	Trenches Loos Section	04/06/1916	15/06/1916
War Diary	Mazingarbe	16/06/1916	24/06/1916
War Diary	Trenches 14 Bis Section	25/06/1916	27/06/1916
War Diary	Trenches 14 Bis	28/06/1916	29/06/1916
War Diary	Trenches 14 Bis Section	30/06/1916	30/06/1916
Heading	War Diary 48th Machine Gun Company 1st. July to 31st July 1916. Volume No 3		
War Diary	Trenches 14 Bis Section	01/07/1916	09/07/1916
War Diary	Mazingarbe	10/07/1916	18/07/1916
War Diary	Trenches Loos Section	19/07/1916	22/07/1916
War Diary	Mazingarbe	23/07/1916	23/07/1916
War Diary	Trenches Hulluch Section	24/07/1916	31/07/1916
Heading	War Diary 48th Machine Gun Company Month Of August 1916. Volume 5		
War Diary	Trenches Hulluch Sector	01/08/1916	22/08/1916
War Diary	Noeux-Les Mines	23/08/1916	24/08/1916
War Diary	Lozinghem	25/08/1916	29/08/1916
War Diary	Corbie	30/08/1916	31/08/1916
Heading	War Diary 48th Machine Gun Company For Month Of September 1916 Volume 5		
War Diary	Sandpit Camp	01/09/1916	03/09/1916
War Diary	Billon Farm	03/09/1916	03/09/1916
War Diary	Carnoy	04/09/1916	04/09/1916
War Diary	Montauban	05/09/1916	11/09/1916
War Diary	Happy Valley Camp	11/09/1916	11/09/1916
War Diary	Corbie	12/09/1916	18/09/1916
War Diary	Allery	19/09/1916	20/09/1916
War Diary	Longpre	21/09/1916	21/09/1916
War Diary	Canada Corner	22/09/1916	23/09/1916
War Diary	Vierstraat Section	24/09/1916	30/09/1916

Type	Description	Start	End
Miscellaneous	Report On Operations Of 48th Infantry Brigade On 9th and 10th September. 1916. in the attack on Guinchy.	15/09/1916	15/09/1916
Heading	War Diary Month Of October 1916 Volume 7 48th Machine Gun Company		
War Diary	Vierstraat Section	01/10/1916	01/11/1916
Heading	War Diary For Month Of November, 1916. Volume 8 48th Machine Gun Company		
Heading	War Diary No 48 Company Machine Gun Corps From 1st November 1916 To 30th November 1916 Vol 8		
War Diary		01/11/1916	09/11/1916
War Diary	Vierstraat Sector	10/11/1916	11/12/1916
Heading	War Diary For Month Of December, 1916 Volume 9 8th Machine Gun Company		
War Diary	Vierstraat Section	01/12/1916	02/12/1916
War Diary	Klondyke Farm	03/12/1916	14/12/1916
War Diary	Vierstraat Section	15/12/1916	31/12/1916
Heading	War Diary for month of January, 1917 Volume 10 48th Machine Gun Company		
Heading	Original War Diary Of 48 M.G. Coy For January 1917		
War Diary	Vierstraat Section	01/01/1917	31/01/1917
Heading	War Diary For Month Of February, 1917 Volume 11 Unit 48th Machine Gun Company		
War Diary	Vierstraat Section	01/02/1917	28/02/1917
Heading	War Diary For Month Of March, 1917 Volume 12 Unit 48th Machine Gun Company		
War Diary	Vierstraat Sector	01/03/1917	18/03/1917
War Diary	Scherpenberg	19/03/1917	30/03/1917
War Diary	Haazbruck	31/03/1917	31/03/1917
Miscellaneous	48 Machine Gun Company Appendix I	17/03/1917	17/03/1917
Operation(al) Order(s)	No 48 Company M.G.C. Operation Order No 15	30/03/1917	30/03/1917
Heading	War Diary For Month Of April, 1917. Volume 13 Unit No 48 Machine Gun Coy		
War Diary	Wizernes	01/04/1917	04/04/1917
War Diary	Recques	05/04/1917	15/04/1917
War Diary	Wizernes	16/04/1917	16/04/1917
War Diary	Brulooze	17/04/1917	17/04/1917
War Diary	28.SW.5a.	18/04/1917	18/04/1917
War Diary	Pioneer Farm N.15. a 1/2 1/2	19/04/1917	19/04/1917
War Diary	Pioneer Farm	19/04/1917	30/04/1917
Operation(al) Order(s)	No 48 Coy. M.G.C. Operation Order No 16	19/04/1917	19/04/1917
Heading	War Diary Volume 14 For Month Of May, 1917 Unit 48th Machine Gun Company		
War Diary	Pioneer Farm	01/05/1917	05/05/1917
War Diary	Klondike Farm	06/05/1917	18/05/1917
War Diary	Vierstraat Sector	19/05/1917	31/05/1917
Operation(al) Order(s)	48 Coy. M.G.C. Operation Order No 23	17/05/1917	17/05/1917
Operation(al) Order(s)	No 48 Machine Gun Coy Operation Order No 22	04/05/1917	04/05/1917
Heading	War Diary For Month Of June, 1917. Volume 5 48th Machine Gun Company		
War Diary	Vierstraat Sector	01/06/1917	02/06/1917
War Diary	Clare Camp	03/06/1917	07/06/1917
War Diary	Vierstraat Sector	07/06/1917	11/06/1917
War Diary	Clare Camp	11/06/1917	12/06/1917
War Diary	Strazeele	13/06/1917	16/06/1917
War Diary	Westoutre	17/06/1917	17/06/1917
War Diary	Strazeele	18/06/1917	19/06/1917

War Diary	St Silvestre	20/06/1917	20/06/1917
War Diary	Cappel	21/06/1917	21/06/1917
War Diary	Rubrouck	22/06/1917	30/06/1917
Operation(al) Order(s)	Operation Order No 24 48 Machine Gun Coy	01/06/1917	01/06/1917
Operation(al) Order(s)	48 Machine Gun Company Operation Order No 28 Appendix II	06/06/1917	06/06/1917
Operation(al) Order(s)	No 48. Coy Machine Gun Corps Operation Order No Appendix III	21/06/1917	21/06/1917
Heading	War Diary For Month Of July, 1917. Volume 16 48th Machine Gun Company		
War Diary	Rubruck	01/07/1917	08/07/1917
War Diary	Tatinghem	09/07/1917	15/07/1917
War Diary	Eringham Area Map Ref. T 29a 4.9. Sheet 19	16/07/1917	21/07/1917
War Diary	Winnezeele Area No 3 I.12.d. 47. Map Ref	22/07/1917	24/07/1917
War Diary	Watou Area Map Ref L15 b 9.1	25/07/1917	25/07/1917
War Diary	Watou	26/07/1917	27/07/1917
War Diary	Watou L15. b. 9.1	28/09/1917	30/09/1917
War Diary	G.11a.6.0	31/07/1917	31/07/1917
Operation(al) Order(s)	No. 48 Coy. M.G.C. Operation Order No 31 Appendix I	07/07/1917	07/07/1917
Operation(al) Order(s)	No. 48 Coy. M.G.C. Operation Order No 33 Appendix 2	15/07/1917	15/07/1917
Operation(al) Order(s)	No. 48 Coy. M.G.C. Operation Order No. 34 Appendix 3	21/07/1917	21/07/1917
Operation(al) Order(s)	No 48 Coy. M.G.C. Operation Order No 35 Appendix 4	24/07/1917	24/07/1917
Operation(al) Order(s)	48 Coy M.G.C. Operation Order No 30 Appendix 5	29/07/1917	29/07/1917
Heading	War Diary For Month Of August, 1917 Volume 17 48th Machine Gun Company		
War Diary	Brandhoek	01/08/1917	09/08/1917
War Diary	H 16 d 62	10/08/1917	14/08/1917
War Diary	Ramparts Yorks	15/08/1917	17/08/1917
War Diary	H 16 d	18/08/1917	18/08/1917
War Diary	Watou "A" Area	19/08/1917	19/08/1917
War Diary	Wormhout	20/08/1917	21/08/1917
War Diary	Courcelles	22/08/1917	26/08/1917
War Diary	Field	27/08/1917	31/08/1917
Miscellaneous	48th Coy M.G.C.	23/08/1917	23/08/1917
Operation(al) Order(s)	48 Coy M.G.C. Operation Order	07/08/1917	07/08/1917
Operation(al) Order(s)	No 48 Coy. M.G.C. Operation Orders No. 39	09/08/1917	09/08/1917
Miscellaneous	No. 48th Coy. M.G.C.	11/05/1917	11/05/1917
Operation(al) Order(s)	48th Machine Gun Company. Operation Order No. 40	14/02/1917	14/02/1917
Miscellaneous	Reference ? map		
Miscellaneous	Appendix B		
Operation(al) Order(s)	48th Machine Gun Company Operation Order No 43	14/08/1917	14/08/1917
Operation(al) Order(s)	48th. Infantry Brigade Order No. 149	17/08/1917	17/08/1917
Miscellaneous	16th Div. No. D.M.G.O. 100/1. 17th August 1917	17/08/1917	17/08/1917
Miscellaneous	16th Div. No. D.M.G.O. 100/3. 17th August 1917	17/08/1917	17/08/1917
Operation(al) Order(s)	16th. Division Administrative Order No. 31	19/08/1917	19/08/1917
Operation(al) Order(s)	48th Infantry Brigade Order No 131	20/08/1917	20/08/1917
Miscellaneous	No 48 Coy. M.G.C. Operation Orders	21/08/1917	21/08/1917
Miscellaneous	Report On The Action Of M.G's 20/11/17	20/11/1917	20/11/1917
Heading	War Diary. For Month Of September 1917. Volume 18 M.G.C. 48th Machine Gun Coy		
War Diary	Croiselles	01/09/1917	30/09/1917
Miscellaneous	16th Div. No. D.M.G.O.140. 11th September 1917	11/09/1917	11/09/1917

Type	Description	Date From	Date To
Miscellaneous	16th Div. No. D.M.G.O. 151. 13th September 1917	13/09/1917	13/09/1917
Operation(al) Order(s)	Operation Order No 7	13/09/1917	13/09/1917
Miscellaneous Operation(al) Order(s)	To Be Attached To Operation Order No 7 Appendix 2	13/09/1917	13/09/1917
Miscellaneous	Appendix 3	13/09/1917	13/09/1917
Miscellaneous	To O.C. B Section	14/09/1917	14/09/1917
Miscellaneous	To OC. 48th M.G. Coy.	16/09/1917	16/09/1917
Miscellaneous	To O.C. 48 M.G. Coy. Report On Minor Operation Of September 15/16 1917	15/09/1917	15/09/1917
Miscellaneous	Report On Division Operation On 15-16/09/17	16/09/1917	16/09/1917
Heading	War Diary For Month Of October 1917 48th Machine Gun Coy Volume Number 19		
War Diary	Croisilles	01/10/1917	14/10/1917
War Diary	Ervillers	15/10/1917	21/10/1917
War Diary	St. Leger	22/10/1917	31/10/1917
Heading	48th Machine Gun Company War Diary For The Month Of November 1917		
War Diary	St. Leger	01/11/1917	07/11/1917
War Diary	Ervillers	08/11/1917	12/11/1917
War Diary	Ervillers	13/10/1917	13/10/1917
War Diary	St. Leger	14/10/1917	19/10/1917
War Diary	Croisilles	20/11/1917	21/11/1917
War Diary	St. Leger	22/11/1917	27/11/1917
War Diary	Ervillers	28/11/1917	30/11/1917
Miscellaneous		23/11/1917	23/11/1917
Heading	48th Machine Gun Company War Diary For The Month Of December 1917		
War Diary	Ervillers	01/12/1917	04/12/1917
War Diary	St. Emilie	05/12/1917	27/12/1917
War Diary	Tincourt	28/12/1917	31/12/1917
Heading	War Diary For Month Of January 1918. Volume 22 Unit 48th Machine Gun Coy. M.G.C.		
War Diary	Tincourt	01/01/1917	02/01/1917
War Diary	St. Emilie	03/01/1918	20/01/1918
War Diary	Tincourt	21/01/1918	30/01/1918
War Diary	St Emilie	31/01/1918	31/01/1918
Operation(al) Order(s)	48 Company M.G.C. Operation Order No 26	08/01/1918	08/01/1918
Operation(al) Order(s)	48 Company M.G.C. Operation Order No 27	19/01/1918	19/01/1918
Operation(al) Order(s)	48 Coy. M.G.C. Operation Order No 28	29/01/1918	29/01/1918
Heading	War Diary For Month Of February 1918 Volume 23 48th Machine Gun Company		
Heading	48th Machine Gun Company War Diary For The Month Of February 1918		
War Diary	Field	01/02/1917	01/02/1917
War Diary	St Emilie	02/02/1918	06/02/1918
War Diary	Villers Faucon	07/02/1918	08/02/1918
War Diary	Field	09/02/1918	09/02/1918
War Diary	(Villers Faucon)	10/02/1918	14/02/1918
War Diary	St Emilie	15/02/1918	18/02/1918
War Diary	Field	19/02/1918	28/02/1918
Operation(al) Order(s)	48 Coy. M.G.C. Operation Order No 29	05/02/1918	05/02/1918
Operation(al) Order(s)	Operation Order No 28 By Lt. C.C. Green Commanding 48 M.G. Coy	14/02/1918	14/02/1918
Miscellaneous	Table "B" Entraining Station. Esquelbecq		
Operation(al) Order(s)	Distribution of 16th. Division Admn. Order 31		

1975/8

Brigade Machine Gun
Company

April 1916 – Feb 1918

16TH DIVISION
48TH INFY BDE

48TH MACHINE GUN COY.
APL 1916-FEB 1918

48 M G Coy/6

VG11

WAR DIARY
or
INTELLIGENCE SUMMARY
(Erase heading not required.)

Army Form C. 2118.

Place	Date	Hour	Summary of Events and Information	Remarks and references to Appendices
GRANTHAM	24-4-16		48 M G Company mobilized for Service Overseas. No issue of the Officers, 10 in number, and at Dunster MD, who mobilized with this Company are as under. There were 143 other ranks.	
			Captain W.T. Blacker Commanding.	
			Lieut P.D. Mulholland 2nd in Command and Transport Officer	
			" W.L. Horan	
			" E.B. Smith	
			" R.P. Cooper	
			" L.D. Fanshawe	
			" M.H. MacLucas	
			" R.C. Hewson	
			" R.H. Bannister	
			" F.H. Derry	

Apl 16
Jul 16

Army Form C. 2118.

WAR DIARY
or
INTELLIGENCE SUMMARY

(Erase heading not required.)

Instructions regarding War Diaries and Intelligence Summaries are contained in F. S. Regs., Part II. and the Staff Manual respectively. Title Pages will be prepared in manuscript.

Place	Date	Hour	Summary of Events and Information	Remarks and references to Appendices
GRANTHAM	25-4-16	12.45am	The Company entrained at GRANTHAM for SOUTHAMPTON. Arrived at SOUTHAMPTON at 3.10pm, Embarked on the CONNAUGHT at 4-30 pm & Sailed for HAVRE at 7.35 pm	
HAVRE	26-4-16	3-30am	Arrived at HAVRE and marched to No 2 Rest Camp about 5 miles from the docks at about 12-30 pm. The night April 26/27th was spent at the camp.	
HAVRE	27-4-16	5-30am	The Company paraded and marched off from No 2 Rest Camp at 5-30 am and entrained at GARE DES MERCHANDISES, HAVRE at 4-30 am.	
NOEUX-LES-MINES	28-4-16	4 am	The Company arrived at NOEUX-LES-MINES and bivouaced Rear the station till about 12 noon and then marched to camp at HOUCHIN arriving about 3 pm. The night April 28/29th was spent in the camp.	

Army Form C. 2118.

WAR DIARY
or
INTELLIGENCE SUMMARY

(Erase heading not required.)

Instructions regarding War Diaries and Intelligence Summaries are contained in F. S. Regs., Part II. and the Staff Manual respectively. Title Pages will be prepared in manuscript.

Place	Date	Hour	Summary of Events and Information	Remarks and references to Appendices
HOUCHIN	29.6.16	12 Noon	The Company received orders from H.Q. 16th Division to report to C.O.C. 49th Infantry Brigade at PHILOSOPHE. On arrival of the Company Ordered 8 guns to go into the the line that night. Positions were reconnoitred by O.C. Company (A section) and at 2.30 pm 4 guns went into the (B section) VILLAGE LINE and 4 in to the GERMAN SWITCH - HULLUCH SECTOR. The night has passed quietly with exception of poisonous gas alarms. All alarms proved to be false.	

Army Form C. 2118.

WAR DIARY
or
INTELLIGENCE SUMMARY

(Erase heading not required.)

Place	Date	Hour	Summary of Events and Information	Remarks and references to Appendices
Trenches Hulluch Sector	30th April 1916		During the day April 30th all was quiet. No guns were fired, but the teams improved their trenches. 'C' & 'D' Sections paraded and marched off to relieve 8 guns of the 35th. M.G. Company in the RESERVE TRENCH, HULLUCH SECTOR. 'C' Section took on emplacements R10, 21, 22 and 23. 'B' Section R14, R25, R27 and S20 in the Support trench.	
PHILOSOPHE	"	7.30pm	During the night April 30th/May 1st there were numerous gas alarms but all were false. Rifle fire In the GERMAN SWITCH rumours of a gas attack from the direction of Loos were heard.	

WAR DIARY or INTELLIGENCE SUMMARY

Army Form C. 2118.

48 MGC
MAY/16

Place	Date	Hour	Summary of Events and Information	Remarks and references to Appendices
TRENCHES HULLUCH SECTION	May 1st	8 a.m.	An enemy's aeroplane was observed from the LONE TREE REDOUBT to fall in the enemy's lines. During the day there was a little sniping about the RESERVE Trench done by the enemy, but no damage was done.	
		4.30 p.m.	Rifle Grenades were fired at HEATED ICAN tea Gun & SRO, but no damage was done. Also the same time an enemy Shell destroyed 2 bays of the RESERVE trench close to the junction of WINGS WAR and RESERVE TRENCH.	
		7.30 p.m.	There was a gas alarm but no gas came. Some enemy's waggons were seen in the distance just off the HULLUCH ROAD. Came not starsy Report from the front line state that several were observed to us. A German Machine Gun was seen firing at one of our aeroplanes but with no result. No. guns of this Company fired during the day.	

2449 Wt. W14957/Mgo 750,000 1/16 J.B.C. & A. Forms/C.2118/12.

Army Form C. 2118.

WAR DIARY
or
INTELLIGENCE SUMMARY

(Erase heading not required.)

Instructions regarding War Diaries and Intelligence Summaries are contained in F. S. Regs., Part II and the Staff Manual respectively. Title Pages will be prepared in manuscript.

Place	Date	Hour	Summary of Events and Information	Remarks and references to Appendices
Mazingarbe TRENCHES HULLUCH SECTION.	May 2nd 1916	11 a.m.	4 9 M.G. Company arrived at PHILOSOPHE to meet guides of 40 M.G. Company. Guides having been detailed 49 M.G. Company started relieving 40 M.G. Company. The last of the relief was over about 9-30 p.m. The Company then marched into billets at NOEUX-LES-MINES arriving about 12 midnight.	
NOEUX-LES MINES	May 3rd		Guns were cleaned and limbers repacked and refitted.	
NOEUX-LES MINES	May 4th		Men were bathed and guns, rifles and equipment inspected.	

WAR DIARY or INTELLIGENCE SUMMARY

Place	Date	Hour	Summary of Events and Information	Remarks and references to Appendices
NOEUX-LES-MINES	May 5th	9 a.m.	Limbers & guns were prepared to go to the trenches.	
		6 p.m.	The Company marched off to PHILOSOPHE to relieve 4.9 M.G. Company.	
		7.30 p.m.	The relief started from PHILOSOPHE and was complete about 4 a.m. The night has passed quietly.	

Army Form C. 2118.

WAR DIARY
or
INTELLIGENCE SUMMARY
(Erase heading not required.)

Instructions regarding War Diaries and Intelligence Summaries are contained in F. S. Regs., Part II and the Staff Manual respectively. Title Pages will be prepared in manuscript.

Place	Date	Hour	Summary of Events and Information	Remarks and references to Appendices
TRENCHES HULLUCH SECTION	May 6th 1916.		The night May 5/6th was passed quietly. Also during May 6th with exception of a little shelling on our RESERVE TRENCH, but no damage was done. Fairly heavy shelling was observed a variable distance along the HOHENZOLLERN REDOUBT just North of us.	
"	May 7th 1916	9-30 a.m.	There was heavy shelling to our left just North of the HULLUCH Road on the Reserve trenches which were reviewed by the brigade on our immediate left.	
		12 noon	There was a false gas alarm in our RESERVE TRENCH. Throughout the day the enemy's artillery was active along the whole of the 4th brigade front. There was a marked absence of aircraft.	

Army Form C. 2118.

WAR DIARY
or
INTELLIGENCE SUMMARY
(Erase heading not required.)

Instructions regarding War Diaries and Intelligence Summaries are contained in F. S. Regs., Part II. and the Staff Manual respectively. Title Pages will be prepared in manuscript.

Place	Date	Hour	Summary of Events and Information	Remarks and references to Appendices
Trenches Hulluch Section	May 8th 1916		The night May 7/8th was passed very quietly also the day May 8th with the exception of a little shelling and some rifle Grenades which landed close to the Gun at S.20 in the support trench	
		8.45 am	5 Germans were observed walking in approximately a S.E. direction across a green field from All a point in the enemy's much line west from the gun position at R.22. A single man went first followed by 4 more in pairs at a considerable distance. The enemy shelled the junction of PONT STREET and TENTH AVENUE.	
		12.45 pm	An enemy's machine gun played on the Gun & Dugout which is just South of the junction of KINGS WAY and NINTH AVENUE.	

Army Form C. 2118.

WAR DIARY
or
INTELLIGENCE SUMMARY
(Erase heading not required.)

Place	Date	Hour	Summary of Events and Information	Remarks and references to Appendices
TRENCHES HULLUCH SECTION	May 9th		Considerable movement behind the enemy's lines was observed. Detachments of Germans were seen moving across the Open Valley away from their trenches. Lewis rifle grenades were fired at the Support Trench. There was a little sniping done by the enemy during the afternoon.	
		1.30 a.m.	The enemy shelled a working party at the Junction of PONT STREET and NINTH AVENUE and again shelled the same spot during the afternoon.	
		10 p.m.	The Artillery on both sides was active during the day in the direction of LOOS. The whole Brigade front in the Reserve Trench was swept by the enemy's machine gun fire. A mine under our front line was observed to go up, but the enemy failed to Occupy the crater.	

2449 Wt. W14957/M90 750,000 1/16 J.B.C. & A. Forms/C.2118/12.

WAR DIARY or INTELLIGENCE SUMMARY

Army Form C. 2118.

Place	Date	Hour	Summary of Events and Information	Remarks and references to Appendices
TRENCHES HULLUCH SECTION	May 10th 1916	11 a.m.	The day has passed quietly with the exception of a heavy Shelling at the Junction of NINTH AVENUE and the HULLUCH ROAD. It lasted about 20 minutes. Indirect fire has been carried out from G.S.I Mtg line X Roads & point K.13.d.6.7 Ref Trench Maps sheet 36.b	
	May 11th 1916	4 P.M. to 9 P.M. 4 P.M.	Hostile mining was suddenly reported by O.C. R.24, R.25 and R.27 Sector north of the Hulluch Road suffering an explosion. Messrs received of hostility of two enemy mines being exploded & succeeded by an enemy raid on the Quarry Sector. The enemy were repulsed of hostile position taken up by our troops in support in WINGSWAY and along HULLUCH ROAD. O.C. above guns instructed to act in conjunction with supporting troops the guns being disposed as follows:- R.24 to watch its front and right, R.25 allotted a defensive position (to WINGSWAY in support of infantry Two R.27 had similar orders to R.25-5.20 ammunition It was evident the front and support were lost when to fasten on M.G. with drawn scheme. If an attack developed north of Hulluch Road the gun would move into WINGSWAY firing North. The © C guns at G.5. 5, 6, 7, 8 leaving also received news of the enemy mines and probable major C assaulted on the Quarry Sector, consulted the O.C. left Sector HULLUCH SECTOR and disposed his guns as follows — G.5.8 moved from its concealed emplacement to an open one at the junction of NINTH AVENUE and WINGSWAY to fire due west across the HULLUCH ROAD. G.5.7 remained in its own emplacement and was to fire north. G.5.6. moved forward position in NINTH AVENUE to a position behind the right parapet (SOUTH) of WINGSWAY to fire across WINGSWAY northwards. G.5.5 moved from its concealed position to a position just north of LONE TREE REDOUBT with instructions not to fire under	
	May 10th 1916	6 P.M.	its not was opened at R.20, R.21, R.22, R.23 with exception of M.G. for protection of M. Guns with O.C. 7th R.I.R. by O.C. above redoubt. Bombing Parties the no damage done R.22 further parapet swept by M.G.	

Army Form C. 2118.

WAR DIARY
or
INTELLIGENCE SUMMARY
(Erase heading not required.)

Instructions regarding War Diaries and Intelligence Summaries are contained in F. S. Regs., Part II. and the Staff Manual respectively. Title Pages will be prepared in manuscript.

Place	Date	Hour	Summary of Events and Information	Remarks and references to Appendices
TRENCHES HULLUCH SECTION	11th May 1916	5.P.M. 4.10 P.M. 7.30 A.M.	Sentry R.12. observed column of smoke apparently rising from Sprais H.26.c 6.5. Ref. Trench map 36°. N.W. 3 Edition 6. O.C. G. 12.34. reports bombardment of TENTH AVENUE on night May 10/11. 500 rounds fired on German trench Sqr. 11.13, 6.39. — 50 rounds fired from G.S. 3 in GERMAN Communication Trench S.E. of HULLUCH Posts N.13. B.15.	Action 6
"	12th May 1916.	— 6.10-7.30 P.M 3-3.30 A.M	Enemy attacked in evening of May 11th and continued in phases all night May 11/12 N.of HULLUCH ROAD. Judging from the sound sin bout appeared to have been attacked at Darrell. Result not known. During the day with exception of a few snaped shots, all quiet. Trenches N. of HULLUCH ROAD and neighbourhood. WINGS WHY and HOLLY LANE suffered Shrapnel fire. Rifle grenades great annoyance + support line of left section HULLUCH Section. Our artillery fired with observed good effect in reply to bombardment of our trenches. 50 rounds sniping fired from G.S. 1 made in Sqr. H.13 d. 3.7. Ref. Trench map 36. N.W. 3 Edition 6. B.12. the target was fixed previously, Corporal Ye Gun R.23. reported bullets which formed behind this and the machine gun in North, with the result that a gun opened to be firing W. or N.W. of POSEN Poser's station afar as the two officers make to examine and ascertain G.S.1. fired 400 rounds aimed on BOIS HUGO. No other guns fired. All guns have operation orders in event of another attack N. of HULLUCH ROAD.	
"	13th MAY 1916		Reports from the G.S. line and RESERVE LINE state that the day passed very quietly.	
"	14th May 1916.	6.P.M. 10.P.M.	Enemy bombardment of trenches N. of HULLUCH ROAD reported by O.C. left section in event of attack developing in West section, between all gun teams ordered to hold themselves in readiness. to O.C. left section HULLUCH section. No guns moved by order. + O.C. left section HULLUCH section. The 11th GERMAN SWITCH night-firing party May 13/14th. The night lay Reserve Trenches day passed quietly during the day. Slight artillery activity N. of HULLUCH ROAD during the day. 13/5.16. Gun G.S. 1 fired 250 rounds and gun G.S. 3. fired 250 rounds indirect on HULLUCH VILLAGE. No other guns fired. No bullets have struck parados at R.23 during night May 12/13th.	

WAR DIARY
or
INTELLIGENCE SUMMARY

(Erase heading not required.)

Army Form C. 2118.

Place	Date	Hour	Summary of Events and Information	Remarks and references to Appendices
TRENCHES HULLUCH Section	15 May 1916.		Slight shelling of RESERVE TRENCH from R.20 to R.23. No damage done. Night of 14/15th square B.6a dug in, also U.S. of POSEN ALLEY. Green S.O.S being placed in battery to screen from aerial observation. Not yet spotted by enemy as no shells have fell near.	
		10.30 a 11.30 p	Gun at G.5.1. fired 250 rounds indirect at BOIS HUGO and G.S.2 fired 250 rounds indirect into HULLUCH VILLAGE at CROSSROADS Sq. H.13.a.2.7.	
TRENCHES Bit 14 SECTION	16th May 1916		Guns H.G. B.g.Coy relieved some guns of 47. M.G. Coy. R.23 went to R.5, R.25 to R.8. and G.5.2 to R.10. Gun left in RESERVE TRENCH by R.23. R.25 & R.24 filled by guns in GERMAN SWITCH. Taking under dugout close to R.25 heard by Oc. Guns at R.6, 20, 21, & 22. Day's Night in RESERVE TRENCH passed quietly. Night of 15/16th May 550 rounds indirect fired at B.g.S.HUGO about pt. Sq. H.25. 0.8.7. where it is reported that German Band is in bad condition. 250 rounds indirect fired at southern end of village HULLUCH pt. Sq. H.13.D.4.0.	
"	17th May 1916	2.2 apm	Reported that night 16/17 & day 17th passed quietly. All guns with exception of slight shelling of RESERVE TRENCH. During night 16/17. 500 rounds indirect fired on BOIS HUGO where enemy working party operation. Rendez. 200 rounds indirect fired on pt. Sq. H.20. A.5.8 where is reported that enemy have a dump.	
"	18th May 1916.	7.30 p.m	The day was spent very quietly. The battery fired a few chance red shells on the RESERVE TRENCH.	
		7 pm	An Enemy Machine Gun always sweeps the parapet of the RESERVE trench at the time. The gun has not yet been located. 500 rounds indirect fire were fired at BOIS HUGO from gun at pt. Ref Trench Map 36cNW3 2/16 500 " " " " " at H.20 & S.8 " " " 1/2	

WAR DIARY
or
INTELLIGENCE SUMMARY

Army Form C. 2118.

Place	Date	Hour	Summary of Events and Information	Remarks and references to Appendices
TRENCHES Bis 14 Section	May 19th 1916	2.30 AM	The day has passed quietly except the enemy shelled the gun emplacement at R7 in the RESERVE TRENCH but it did not last long and have done no damage done. 500 rounds indirect fire was fired at H2.5 a3.1 Ref Trench Map 36a N.W.3 SDDitron 6 during the night May 18/19 by the gun at R1. - The enemy has reported to have working parties in front Spot. 500 rounds indirect fire were also fired from V2 at H2.0, a 5.8 www Ref Trench Map 36 c.N.W.3 SDDitron 6	

WAR DIARY or INTELLIGENCE SUMMARY

Army Form C. 2118.

Place	Date	Hour	Summary of Events and Information	Remarks and references to Appendices
TRENCHES R1 S 14 SECTION	May 20. 1916	6.30 pm	The enemy shelled the RESERVE Trench between POSEN ALLEY and RAILWAY ALLEY at 6-30 but no damage was done.	
			An enemy machine gun played on the parapet at M.G. R.9 in GUN ALLEY during the night May 19/20th.	
		9.45 pm	500 rounds indirect fire were fired from R.7 into the village of BENIFONTAINE.	
		9.55 pm	500 rounds indirect fire were fired from R.6 also at BENIFONTAINE. The enemy replied by browning the parapet of the RESERVE Trench with a machine gun.	
		10.45 pm	R.7 was shelled.	

Army Form C. 2118.

WAR DIARY
or
INTELLIGENCE SUMMARY
(Erase heading not required.)

Place	Date	Hour	Summary of Events and Information	Remarks and references to Appendices
TRENCHES Bis 14 SECTION	May 21 1916		There was a good deal of shelling by the enemy in the RESERVE during the day and also in GUN ALLEY and especially in LOOS. One shell wounded 3 men, 1 seriously, at the gun position R4 and a shell	
		9.30 pm	was blown in at R5. The sentry at R7 placed a German cine-matograph (believed to be). One of our snipers at top of R.S. 14 where a sniper is thought to be. One of our snipers fired 18 shots at them and they disappeared. About 15 minutes later the same appeared and apparently altogether into a dug out. There were a number of GERMAN aeroplanes over LOOS during the evening. Indirect fire was fired at the crossroads in REMI FONTAINE Ref Trench Map 36" N.W. Edition 6 also at B15.16 and HULLUCH S.	

Army Form C. 2118.

WAR DIARY
or
INTELLIGENCE SUMMARY

(Erase heading not required.)

Instructions regarding War Diaries and Intelligence Summaries are contained in F. S. Regs., Part II and the Staff Manual respectively. Title Pages will be prepared in manuscript.

Place	Date	Hour	Summary of Events and Information	Remarks and references to Appendices
TRENCHES 16 Bis SECTION.	May 22nd 1916		An enemy Machine Gun in his front line was observed and East of trench H25.6 Ref Trench Map 36cNW. 29.6. The artillery was informed and fired with effect on that spot. The enemy's artillery was particularly active during the day, some big shells falling about RAILWAY.	
		12.30am	There was a Gas alarm but it was false.	
		10.30pm	The enemy threw a search light over our lines to find aeroplanes which were heard overhead. The EOON TOWER was shelled but quite 50% of the shells did not go off. Indirect fire was tried at 16 Bis and H20, H5.0 Ref Trench Map 36cNW. 22.16 during the May 21/22.	

Army Form C. 2118.

WAR DIARY
or
INTELLIGENCE SUMMARY
(Erase heading not required.)

Place	Date	Hour	Summary of Events and Information	Remarks and references to Appendices
TRENCHES R13 14 SECTION	May 23rd		The day has passed particularly quietly with nothing to report except a little shelling of the RESERVE TRENCH by the enemy at the junction of RAILWAY ALLEY and RESERVE TRENCH.	
		5am	'C' Section went to Loos to relieve a gun of 47 M.G. Company in the Loos defences.	
		4pm	'D' Section went to Loos to relieve a gun of 47 M.G. Company in the Loos defences.	

WAR DIARY
or
INTELLIGENCE SUMMARY

Army Form C. 2118.

Place	Date	Hour	Summary of Events and Information	Remarks and references to Appendices
Ruitz Bis 14. SECTION	May 24th 1916		The day was spent quietly on the whole. The gun at R.7 fired on a large working party and small item later on. The battery retaliated with shrapnel. A & B Section. The Company were relieved by 47 M.G. Company on the night of the 24th/25th May. C & D Section relieved 8 guns of 47 M.G. Company.	
		4 AM	The relief was complete at about 4 am. and A & B Section marched back to billets at Noeux-Les-Mines arriving about 6 am.	
NOEUX-LES-MINES	May 25th 1916		The day was spent cleaning guns and equipment and the men had a bath.	
		4 pm	The Village was shelled between 4 pm & 4-30 pm.	

Army Form C. 2118.

WAR DIARY
or
INTELLIGENCE SUMMARY

(Erase heading not required.)

Instructions regarding War Diaries and Intelligence Summaries are contained in F. S. Regs., Part II. and the Staff Manual respectively. Title Pages will be prepared in manuscript.

Place	Date	Hour	Summary of Events and Information	Remarks and references to Appendices
NOEUX-LES-MINES	May 26th 1916		The day was spent in training in Machine Gun work.	
			The village was shelled for about half an hour but few shells were fired.	
"	May 27/28th 1916	2·30 pm	The day spent in training in Machine Gun work. The Company received news from 48th Brigade HQ. to be ready to move off in half an hour. Guns & ammunition were at once packed on the limbers and A & B Sections moved	
		6·30 pm	off with Company H.Q. at 6-30 p.m. B' Section went to Loos & came under command of O.C. LOOS defences. A' Section sent 2 guns to the 65 METRE REDOUBT & (w) NORTHERN SAP REDOUBT. (x) HQ remained at PHILOSOPHE	
TRENCHES 16 BIS SECTION	May 28th 1916	8 pm	The night 27/28th was passed very quietly, also the day May 28th. The 2 guns from NORTHERN SAP REDOUBT changed their position to V8 & V9 in the VILLAGE Line and the 2 guns from 65 METRE REDOUBT changed their position to V11 & V12.	
TRENCHES 16 BIS SECTION	May 29th 1916		The day was passed very quietly with the exception of a few occasional shells. 'B', 'C' & 'D' Sections report that the situation in Loos is quiet & normal. 'A' Section in the VILLAGE LINE reconnoitred trees been	

Army Form C. 2118.

WAR DIARY
or
INTELLIGENCE SUMMARY

(Erase heading not required.)

Instructions regarding War Diaries and Intelligence Summaries are contained in F. S. Regs., Part II. and the Staff Manual respectively. Title Pages will be prepared in manuscript.

Place	Date	Hour	Summary of Events and Information	Remarks and references to Appendices
TRENCHES 16 Bris "A" SECTION	May 30th 1916		The guns (A Section) in the VILLAGE remained in their same positions and the night 29/30th May and the 30th May has passed very quietly.	
TRENCHES 16 Bris "A" Section	May 31st 1916		A new M.G. emplacement made by "A" Section has been shelled but little damage had done. The two guns in that spot spent a quiet day but for this slight shelling.	
Trenches Loos Section	"	12·45	The 2 guns of 'A' Section (one in the PRYETE REDOUBT & one on the LENS ROAD) spent a quiet day except for half hour shelling at the PRYETE REDOUBT between 12·45 and 1·15 pm.	

J.M.Maclean Major
O.C. 16 M.G. Company

31 – 5 – 16.

Army Form C. 2118.

WAR DIARY
or
INTELLIGENCE SUMMARY

(Erase heading not required.)

Vol 2
48 M G Coy
XVI

Place	Date	Hour	Summary of Events and Information	Remarks and references to Appendices
TRENCHES 14 R.I.S Section of LOOS SECTOR	June 1st 1916		A Section in the VILLAGE line spent a very quiet day and also a very quiet night 31 May/June 1st. There was a good deal aircraft activity during the day.	June
TRENCHES LOOS Section A.I.S BATTN 1916	June 2nd 1916		The Company relieved 40 M.G. Company in the LOOS SECTOR. Relief started in the afternoon and was complete by 12 mid night. The Company now occupy 2 gun position in the SUPPORT line, 2 in the RESERVE LINE, 2 in the LOOS DEFENCES, 2 in the LENS REDOUBT and 2 in the VILLAGE south of the LENS - BETHUNE ROAD. The enemy's artillery was active at LOOS.	

Army Form C. 2118.

WAR DIARY
or
INTELLIGENCE SUMMARY

(Erase heading not required.)

Place	Date	Hour	Summary of Events and Information	Remarks and references to Appendices
TRENCHES LOOS SECTION	June 3rd 1916.		The enemy shelled ENCLOSURE AVENUE in the RESERVE Trench between 5 & 6 p.m. but little damage was done. The Reserve Trench South of ENGLISH ALLEY was shelled off & on throughout the night June 2nd/3rd & Saturday June 3rd. One man of the Company was wounded. The LE JOIE ROAD was shelled at RUSTUM and GYAN at 6 p.m. The 2 front line SUPPORT Trench were not drawn to the RESERVE Trench	
TRENCHES LOOS SECTION	June 4th 1916.		The enemy's artillery was active about LOOS and FOSSE 7 was heavily shelled between 9 a.m. & 10 a.m. The guns to the VILLAGE LINE spent a quiet day.	

Army Form C. 2118.

WAR DIARY
or
INTELLIGENCE SUMMARY

(Erase heading not required.)

Instructions regarding War Diaries and Intelligence
Summaries are contained in F. S. Regs., Part II
and the Staff Manual respectively. Title Pages
will be prepared in manuscript.

Place	Date	Hour	Summary of Events and Information	Remarks and references to Appendices
Trenches Loos Section	June 5th 1916		Enemy's artillery was on whole active about Loos and they dropped shells very close to "A"section's left but did no damage. The enemy's Snipers were also very active. The day was spent very quietly in LENS REDOUBT and VILLAGE LINE.	
Trenches Loos Section	June 6th 1916		The day was spent quietly except for a little shelling on Loos.	
Trenches Loos Section	June 7th 1916		The lanes behind the RESERVE Trench were shelled intermittently during this day, but no material damage was done. The enemy's machine guns were active during the night June 6/7. The guns in the VILLAGE LINE spent a very quiet day.	

WAR DIARY or INTELLIGENCE SUMMARY

Army Form C. 2118.

Place	Date	Hour	Summary of Events and Information	Remarks and references to Appendices
TRENCHES LOOS SECTION	June 8th 1916.		There was the usual amount of shelling in the RESERVE Trenches East of Loos. No damage has come. Otherwise the day was spent very quietly. The village of MAZINGARBE was shelled between 1 and 2 p.m.	
TRENCHES LOOS SECTION	June 9th 1916.		The enemy and his usual amount of shelling on the lines behind the Reserve line in Loos. Owing to a change in the wind in the evening a gas alert was ordered.	
TRENCHES LOOS SECTION	June 10th 1916.		The day was spent very quietly owing to heavy rain which went on most of the day. There was a little shelling on the houses behind the houses behind the RESERVE TRENCH at LOOS.	

Army Form C. 2118.

WAR DIARY
or
INTELLIGENCE SUMMARY

(Erase heading not required.)

Place	Date	Hour	Summary of Events and Information	Remarks and references to Appendices
TRENCHES LOOS SECTION	June 11th 1916		The day was quiet with the exception of a little shelling round the RESERVE TRENCH. 500 rounds indirect fire were fired from G.36.a & 8.6 in to the enemy trench in H.26.c. and H.29.d. at 11-20 p.m.	
TRENCHES LOOS SECTION	June 12th 1916		The day was quite normal. ENCLOSURE AVENUE occupied by R. Section was shelled during the afternoon but no damage was done. The weather during the day was very inclement.	
"	June 13th 1916		The enemy shelled the houses behind the RESERVE TRENCH in LOOS intermittently during the day. He did little damage, but prevented work in the trench from going on. The weather was very wet and misty.	

Army Form C. 2118.

WAR DIARY
or
INTELLIGENCE SUMMARY

(Erase heading not required.)

Instructions regarding War Diaries and Intelligence Summaries are contained in F. S. Regs., Part II. and the Staff Manual respectively. Title Pages will be prepared in manuscript.

Place	Date	Hour	Summary of Events and Information	Remarks and references to Appendices
TRENCHES LOOS SECTION	June 14th 1916		The enemy shelled the trenches behind the RESERVE TRENCH in two as usual during the afternoon, but little damage was done. 500 rounds in direct fire was fired on the enemy's trench at 10.30 pm in the enemy's trench H.26, & Ref Trench map 36° N.W S23.5.6	
"	June 15th 1916		250 rounds indirect fire was fired at the enemy's trenches in square G.H.26 & Ref Trench map 36° N.W S23.5.6 between 10 pm. and 12 pm. midnight. The enemy replied with 2 or 3 shells but appeared to have no definite aim. The road running East and West in Loos at G.26.d was shelled during the afternoon on the 15th June. The German Machine guns were active during the night 14/15 June.	

2449 Wt W14957/Mg0 750,000 1/16 J.B.C. & A. Forms/C.2118/12.

Army Form C. 2118.

WAR DIARY
or
INTELLIGENCE SUMMARY

(Erase heading not required.)

Place	Date	Hour	Summary of Events and Information	Remarks and references to Appendices
MAZINGARBE	June 16th 1916.		The Company was relieved by 47 M.G. Company during the day. 'A' and 'C' Section to Kedrew into billets at MAZINGARBE arriving 17-6-16. 'B' & 'D' Sections went into the Loos defences and at 12-30 A.M. a came under the orders of the Commandant, Loos.	
"	June 17th 1916.		The half Company (A and C Sections) in billets spent the day in cleaning the guns and their equipment and in the afternoon had a 0 bath	
"	June 18th 1916		The day was spent in training in mechanism, Immediate action and Anti. Practise in the use of gas helmets was also done.	

Army Form C. 2118.

WAR DIARY
or
INTELLIGENCE SUMMARY

(Erase heading not required.)

Instructions regarding War Diaries and Intelligence Summaries are contained in F. S. Regs., Part II and the Staff Manual respectively. Title Pages will be prepared in manuscript.

Place	Date	Hour	Summary of Events and Information	Remarks and references to Appendices
MAZINGARBE	June 19th 1916		The day was spent in the training of the men in Machine Gun work in Reduction and Immediate action.	
		7.30pm	'A' and 'C' Sections marched to Loos to relieve B & D Sections in the Loos Defences	
"	June 20th 1916	12.30AM	'B' and 'D' Sections arrived from Loos.	
		6AM.	The two Sections went to have a bath. The rest of the day was spent cleaning guns and equipment.	
"	June 21st		The day was spent in training in Machine Gun work and cleaning gun.	
"	June 22nd		The day was spent in training in Machine Gun work. At 5pm the Company had orders to be ready to move in half an hour. Notice was up to hour No more orders had been received	

WAR DIARY or INTELLIGENCE SUMMARY

Army Form C. 2118.

Place	Date	Hour	Summary of Events and Information	Remarks and references to Appendices
MAZINGARBE	June 23 1916		The day was spent in training machine gun teams including drill with limber. The half an hour notice to move was cancelled.	
MAZINGARBE	June 24 1916	9 p.m.	The day was spent training the men in mechanism, and drill. Two gun teams of 'B' Section went up to relieve two guns of the 49 M.G. Coy in the NORTHERN SAP REDOUBT AND 65 METRE POINT REDOUBT.	
TRENCHES 14 Bis SECTION	June 25 1916	7 A.M.	The two remaining gun teams of 'B' Section and 'D' Section went up to the trenches to relieve guns of 49 M.G. Company in the VILLAGE LINE, CHALK PIT ALLEY & GUN TRENCH. Two Sections of 49 M.G. Coy having been relieved they went to LOOS to relieve 'A' & 'C' Sections. 'A' & 'C' Sections then proceeded to the RESERVE TRENCH and took up new positions in the remaining 2 Sections of 49 M.G. Coy. Indirect fire was opened on the enemy's communication trenches. Gas was to have been discharged together with an artillery bombardment followed by a wire cutting raid. Machine Guns were to have fired between Machine Gun fire and an infantry raid, but the raid did not come off as the wind was unsuitable for the discharge of gas. Hence there was indirect M.G. fire done during the night.	

WAR DIARY
or
INTELLIGENCE SUMMARY

Army Form C. 2118.

Place	Date	Hour	Summary of Events and Information	Remarks and references to Appendices
TRENCHES 16 Bn SECTION	June 26th 1916		4000 rounds were at the enemy's communication trench during the night 25/26th. The day on the whole has been fairly quiet. Heavy enemy shelling of the REDERIE TRENCH between 11 A.M. & 12 noon. The trench was blown in at one point but our L.T.M. battery damage was done.	
TRENCHES 16 Bn SECTION	June 27th 1916		On the night of the 26/27 June a direct fire was opened all night on the enemy's communication trenches. About 1000 rounds were expended. The day 27 June has been spent fairly quietly with the exception of a little shelling by the enemy in the early hours of the morning. Orders were received at 5 p.m. that the 51st Division gas & smoke attack would take place about the evening of the 28th instant, and the hours and men from "A" Company, and "C" Coy were detailed to look after gas & the night of the Enemy's Communication trenches.	

WAR DIARY or INTELLIGENCE SUMMARY

Army Form C. 2118.

Place	Date	Hour	Summary of Events and Information	Remarks and references to Appendices
TRENCHES 14 Bis	June 28th 1916.		Our artillery was active at intervals throughout the night, but the enemy made very little retaliation. During the night 28/29th Lieutenant ___ of the enemy's Communication Trenches by the Company. At 10 p.m. rifle and machine gun fire was opened on the enemy all down the divisional front for 2 minutes. Trench mortars and artillery also followed and the Machine Gun Section cooperated with the french mortars.	
	June 29th 1916		After this indirect fire on the night of 28/29th June the enemy retaliated with some violence at the junction of CHALK PIT ALLEY and RESERVE TRENCH, but little damage was done. Also at the junction of BROADWAY and RESERVE TRENCH where the battle emplacement was slightly damaged. The day, otherwise was spent quietly. Our artillery was active throughout the day.	

Army Form C. 2118.

WAR DIARY
or
INTELLIGENCE SUMMARY

(Erase heading not required.)

Instructions regarding War Diaries and Intelligence Summaries are contained in F. S. Regs., Part II. and the Staff Manual respectively. Title Pages will be prepared in manuscript.

Place	Date	Hour	Summary of Events and Information	Remarks and references to Appendices
TRENCHES 14 Bis SECTION	June 30th		During the night 29th/30th June Lichyer fire was carried out on the enemy's communication trenches and roads. The day was spent very quietly with the exception of a few shells fired at CON TRENCH which damaged our emplacement. Our artillery was very active throughout the day.	

M. Mackie Major
O.C. 40 M.G. Company.

2449 Wt. W14957/M90 750,000 1/16 J.B.C. & A. Forms/C.2118/12.

W A R   D I A R Y

48th Machine Gun Company

1st. July to 31st. July 1916.

VOLUME No. 3.

Army Form C. 2118.

WAR DIARY
or
INTELLIGENCE SUMMARY

(Erase heading not required.)

Place	Date	Hour	Summary of Events and Information	Remarks and references to Appendices
TRENCHES 14 Bis SECTION	July 1st 1916.		The day was spent quietly in our front. The GERMAN Trench Guns were active between 4 and 9-30 p.m., but did no damage. Orders were received from Brigade H.Q. that during the day that there will be a raid on the enemy's trenches carried out during the night 1/2 July under a smoke cloud if the weather was suitable, and the machine gun were to cooperate by firing indirect on Enemy communication trenches behind the portion of the enemy's trenches to be raided, but the operation was cancelled on account of unsuitable weather conditions. However the machine gun Carried out indirect fire through out the night.	

Army Form C. 2118.

WAR DIARY
or
INTELLIGENCE SUMMARY

(Erase heading not required.)

Place	Date	Hour	Summary of Events and Information	Remarks and references to Appendices
TRENCHES 14 BIS SECTION	July 2nd 1916		Indirect fire carried out during the night 2/3 July on the enemy's communication trenches, tracks and roads especially between 12-30AM and 1-15 AM. when they were cooperating with the a raid made by the infantry on the enemy's front line trench. The day was spent quietly except about 10 p.m. when CHALK PIT ALLEY was shelled with shrapnel in retaliation to our artillery fire. Wounded one man.	
"	July 3rd 1916		The day was passed quietly except between 10 and 11 p.m. when the RESERVE TRENCH was shelled. The usual indirect fire was carried on on the enemy's communication trenches, tracks and the street of HULLUCH during the night July 3/4.	

Army Form C. 2118.

● WAR DIARY ●
or
INTELLIGENCE SUMMARY

(Erase heading not required.)

Place	Date	Hour	Summary of Events and Information	Remarks and references to Appendices
TRENCHES 14 Bis SECTION	July 4th 1916		The day was spent particularly quietly. Indirect fire was at about carried on on the enemy's communications during the night 3/4th July. Preparations to assist in a raid on the German trenches by the Infantry were made, but the raid was put off on account of weather conditions.	
"	July 5th 1916		Nothing of particular importance happened during the day. Our artillery was active. Indirect fire was carried out during the night 4/5 July on the enemy's communications.	

Army Form C. 2118.

WAR DIARY
or
INTELLIGENCE SUMMARY

(Erase heading not required.)

Instructions regarding War Diaries and Intelligence Summaries are contained in F.S. Regs., Part II. and the Staff Manual respectively. Title Pages will be prepared in manuscript.

Place	Date	Hour	Summary of Events and Information	Remarks and references to Appendices
TRENCHES H.31.5 SECTION	July 6th 1916		At 2.45 pm the RESERVE trench was bombarded till 3 pm the heavy L.G. the Observation Post Aug 631 being heavy. The usual indirect fire was carried out during the night of the 6/7 July.	
"	July 7 1916		The day was about equally with the exception of 2 O.P. shelling in the RESERVE TRENCH. Indications from our canteen roughly throughout 6/7 July & the enemy's communication trenches were more front trench than it was likely that trenches which could serve to and the study of HULLUCH	

Army Form C. 2118.

WAR DIARY
or
INTELLIGENCE SUMMARY

(Erase heading not required.)

Instructions regarding War Diaries and Intelligence Summaries are contained in F. S. Regs., Part II and the Staff Manual respectively. Title Pages will be prepared in manuscript.

Place	Date	Hour	Summary of Events and Information	Remarks and references to Appendices
TRENCHES In B15 SECTION	July 8th 1916		The day was spent particularly quietly. Indirect fire was carried out during the night 7/8 July on the enemy's communication trenches, tracks and roads, also on to the VILLAGE of HULLUCH.	
"	July 9th 1916		Nothing of importance happened during the day. Rane was very little shelling. At 9.30 p.m. a German aeroplane came over as far as the RESERVE trench and dropped a bomb, but did not damage. Indirect fire was carried on enemy's communication trenches behind the enemy's lines which were reported by a prisoner to be eventually used as a relief. On the night 9/10 July 'B' & 'D' sections were relieved by 2 Sections of 47 M.G. Company.	

Army Form C. 2118.

WAR DIARY
or
INTELLIGENCE SUMMARY

(Erase heading not required.)

Place	Date	Hour	Summary of Events and Information	Remarks and references to Appendices
MAZINGARBE	July 10th 1916		'B' & 'D' Sections having been relieved proceeded to Loos at 7 AM to take over 'A' Keep, one gun of 'B', Keep West and 'C' Keep Loos defences from 2 sections of 47 M.G. Company and when this came under orders of the Commandant of Loos. The 2 sections of 47 M.G. Company then went to the RESERVE Trench and relieved 'A' 'C' Sections in '14 Bis Section'. 'A' 'C' and 'D' withdrew to billets at MAZINGARBE, 'A' Section arriving at 1 am 11-7-16. and 'C' at 9 pm 10-7-16.	
MAZINGARBE	July 11th 1916		The day was spent in cleaning guns and equipment. At 1 pm orders were received to withdraw 'B' & 'D' Sections from Loos back to MAZINGARBE. Preparations were made for this	

Army Form C. 2118.

WAR DIARY
or
INTELLIGENCE SUMMARY

(Erase heading not required.)

Place	Date	Hour	Summary of Events and Information	Remarks and references to Appendices
MAZINGARBE	July 12th 1916		At 2 am 'B' & 'D' Sections arrived from Loos and went to billets. The day was spent in cleaning up equipment & guns and batteries were told off. There was an inspection of clothing.	
"	July 13th 1916		The Company marched to NOEUX-LES-MINES to pack and clean limbers. They returned to MAZINGARBE about 3.30. At 5.30pm there was an inspection parade and practice in handling guns.	
"	July 14 1916		The morning was spent at an inspection by the G.O.C. 48 Infantry Brigade. The afternoon and evening was spent cleaning equipment.	
"	July 15 1916	10.30AM	The Company went for a route march and had dinners in the field and returned to billets at 5 pm.	

Army Form C. 2118.

WAR DIARY
or
INTELLIGENCE SUMMARY

(Erase heading not required.)

Instructions regarding War Diaries and Intelligence Summaries are contained in F. S. Regs., Part II. and the Staff Manual respectively. Title Pages will be prepared in manuscript.

Place	Date	Hour	Summary of Events and Information	Remarks and references to Appendices
MAZINGARBE	16 July 1916		The day was spent cleaning guns, Ammunition and equipment.	
"	17 July 1916		All guns &c were overhauled and Ammunition was cleaned in belt boxes	
"	18 July 1916		During the morning equipment was inspected and in the evening the Company moved off to relieve 49 M.G. Company in the LOOS Section. A + B Sections going to the RESERVE TRENCH and 'B' Section the LOOS Defences and "C" Section to the VILLAGE LINE. The relief was complete by 2 am 19th July.	

Army Form C. 2118.

WAR DIARY
or
INTELLIGENCE SUMMARY

(Erase heading not required.)

Instructions regarding War Diaries and Intelligence Summaries are contained in F. S. Regs, Part II. and the Staff Manual respectively. Title Pages will be prepared in manuscript.

Place	Date	Hour	Summary of Events and Information	Remarks and references to Appendices
TRENCHES LOOS SECTION	19 July 1916		The enemy's artillery was fairly active during the day in LOOS VILLAGE, but did not do very much damage. Indirect fire was carried out during the night 18/19 July on the enemy's communications and also during the day (q.v.) on the enemy's communications and also for instruction of the men attached for instruction.	
"	20 July 1916		The RESERVE TRENCH was heavily shelled at intervals during the day but little damage was done. Indirect fire was carried out during the night 19/20 July on the enemy's communication trenches.	
"	21 July 1916	4pm	Indirect was carried out as usual during the night 20/21 July on the enemy's communication trenches and suspected mm. and RE dumps behind their lines. The RESERVE trench in the left subsection was heavily shelled for a short time.	

Army Form C. 2118.

● WAR DIARY
or
INTELLIGENCE SUMMARY

(Erase heading not required.)

Instructions regarding War Diaries and Intelligence Summaries are contained in F. S. Regs., Part II and the Staff Manual respectively. Title Pages will be prepared in manuscript.

Place	Date	Hour	Summary of Events and Information	Remarks and references to Appendices
TRENCHES LOOS SECTION	July 22nd 1916		The Company was relieved by 121 M.G. Company during the afternoon with the exception of the 3 guns of "D" Section in the Loos Defences.	
		9.30pm	Those relieved withdrew to MAZINGARBE in billets.	
MAZINGARBE	July 23rd 1916		Rec'd proceeded again to the trenches to take over from 49 M.G. Company in the HULLUCH SECTION.	
			The day was spent clearing up front and equipment and the officers reconnoitred the HULLUCH SECTION.	
		9pm	The Company marched off to relieve the 49 M.G. Company in the HULLUCH SECTION.	
TRENCHES HULLUCH SECTION	July 24 1916	8	By 12 midnight the Company had relieved 49 M.G. Company in the night of 23/24 July. The day has been very quiet. Enemy & Sniper been active but there was little shelling.	

Army Form C. 2118.

WAR DIARY
or
INTELLIGENCE SUMMARY

(Erase heading not required.)

Instructions regarding War Diaries and Intelligence Summaries are contained in F. S. Regs., Part II. and the Staff Manual respectively. Title Pages will be prepared in manuscript.

Place	Date	Hour	Summary of Events and Information	Remarks and references to Appendices
TRENCHES HULLUCH SECTION.	25th July 1916		Indirect fire was carried out during the night 24/25 July on the enemy's communication trenches. The day, 25th July, has been very quietly.	
"	26 July 1916		During the night 25/26 July the enemy's snipers and Mn.Gs were active. Indirect fire was carried out on the enemy communication trenches, tracks & light railways known to be used for carrying rations and used for relief. The day was very quiet.	
"	27 July 1916		The day & night was spent very quietly in the RESERVE Trench. Indirect fire was carried on during the night 26/27 July on the enemy's communications.	

2449 Wt. W14957/M90 750,000 1/16 J.B.C. & A. Forms/C.2118/12.

Army Form C. 2118.

WAR DIARY
or
INTELLIGENCE SUMMARY

(Erase heading not required.)

Instructions regarding War Diaries and Intelligence Summaries are contained in F. S. Regs., Part II. and the Staff Manual respectively. Title Pages will be prepared in manuscript.

Place	Date	Hour	Summary of Events and Information	Remarks and references to Appendices
TRENCHES HULLUCH SECTION	July 28th 1916		Indirect fire was carried out on the enemy's communications during the night 28/29 July. The 28th July was very quiet.	
"	July 29th		Hostile artillery was very active during the day, also trench and machine guns during night 28/29 July. Heavy aeroplane was also fairly active. Indirect fire was carried out during the night 28/29 July as usual.	
"	July 30th		Indirect fire was carried out during the night 29/30 July on communication trenches behind the enemy's lines, and also for a short time during the day at a trench which had been to be occupied but the result could not be seen. The day was passed with no incident of importance.	

2449 Wt. W14957/M90 750,000 1/16 J.B.C. & A. Forms/C.2118/12.

Army Form C. 2118.

WAR DIARY
or
INTELLIGENCE SUMMARY

(Erase heading not required.)

Place	Date	Hour	Summary of Events and Information	Remarks and references to Appendices
TRENCHES HULLUCH "B" SECTION	July 31st		The enemy's M.G.s and snipers were less active during the night 30/31 July. Our artillery was active at intervals during the day. Two Germans were seen from a M.G. observation post carrying planks in a trolley line which has recently been laid. Indirect fire was carried on the enemy's communications at Wood during the night 30/31 July.	

J.P.Blacker Major.
O.C. 48 M.G. Company

Vol 4

WAR DIARY.

148th Machine Gun Company

MONTH OF AUGUST, 1916.

VOLUME:- 5

Army Form C. 2118.

WAR DIARY
or
INTELLIGENCE SUMMARY

(Erase heading not required.)

48 Machine Gun Company

Place	Date	Hour	Summary of Events and Information	Remarks and references to Appendices
TRENCHES HULLUCH SECTOR	August 1st 1916		The day was spent quietly. The enemy's T.Ms. traversed the parapet of Reserve Trench but no damage was done. Indirect fire was carried out during the night 31 July/Aug 1st on the enemy's communication Trenches and light railways	
"	August 2nd 1916		At 6 a.m. 2.8.16 a hostile aeroplane dropped bombs on our Reserve Trench between the M.G. position R2 and R4 and at 2 p.m. dropped another behind the Reserve Trench. R2 on an instance machine fired a drum at our support and Reserve lines. The enemy's M.G. were very active at great's he replied in CITE ST ELIE and interferences to miniature Indirect fire was carried out in many other places during the night 1-2 August.	

WAR DIARY
or
INTELLIGENCE SUMMARY

Army Form C. 2118.

Place	Date	Hour	Summary of Events and Information	Remarks and references to Appendices
TRENCHES HULLUCH SECTION	August 3rd 1916.		There was a good deal of Trench Mortar activity early in the morning. Our artillery was active at intervals throughout the day. At 2-30 p.m. and 6-45 p.m. a hostile aeroplane came over our lines. The latter dropped bombs on Some Hill gun emplacements but did no damage. The usual amount of Machine gun & direct fire was carried out during the night 2/3 August on the enemy's communications.	
	Aug 4th 1916		There was a certain amount of artillery activity during the day, but the enemy's artillery was particularly quiet. The enemy's transport was heard just east of PT 5E1E. Indirect fire was turned on in the enemy's roads & tracks during the night 3/4 August.	

Army Form C. 2118.

WAR DIARY
or
INTELLIGENCE SUMMARY.
(Erase heading not required.)

Instructions regarding War Diaries and Intelligence Summaries are contained in F. S. Regs., Part II. and the Staff Manual respectively. Title pages will be prepared in manuscript.

Place	Date	Hour	Summary of Events and Information	Remarks and references to Appendices
Trenches HULLUCH SECTION	Aug 5th 1916	1.0 AM	There was a raid on the GERMAN front line carried out by the 10th Infantry Brigade. The 8th M.G. opened fire indirect fire on the enemy Communication trenches when the artillery barrage commenced and kept it up for about an hour. After the raid had further the fire was brought to bear on the roads and tracks behind the enemy's lines. The day was fairly quiet after the early hours of the morning.	
"	Aug 6th 1916		The night 5/6 August was very quiet with the exception of the usual sniping and M.G. fire by the enemy. At 12 midnight a large fire had been broken out in the direction of DOURIN. One of our aeroplanes having previously passed over our lines. Between 10 and 1 pm the enemy shelled our Reserve Trench hearing it in 2 places. Indirect fire was carried out by M.Gs on 8 different places behind the enemy lines including roads, light railways, back end communication trenches	

Army Form C. 2118.

WAR DIARY
or
INTELLIGENCE SUMMARY.
(Erase heading not required.)

Place	Date	Hour	Summary of Events and Information	Remarks and references to Appendices
TRENCHES HULLUCH SECTION H6	Aug 7th		Early on the night of 6/7th August the enemy opened a rapid m.g fire. Very soon after our m.gs started to fire. The enemy died very quick. All night the usual indirect fire and close elong fire against front to a change in the boundaries in the Hulluch 'A' and 'B' Section, North of the Hulluch Road were relieved by 2/4 M.G. Coy at 5.7 p.m. 'B' Patron withdrew to the cellars at NOEUX-LES-MINES and 'A' Section remained in the village there & so that it was handy to go and take up the area from 4.9 M.G. Coy on the night of D Section then occupying the 2 new Hulluch Section from LE RUTOIRE ALLEY to POSEN ALLEY. 'C' Section occupied the posters in the village line.	

Army Form C. 2118.

WAR DIARY
or
INTELLIGENCE SUMMARY.
(Erase heading not required.)

Place	Date	Hour	Summary of Events and Information	Remarks and references to Appendices
TRENCHES Hollot Section	Aug 8th 1916		"A" Section went up to the RESERVE TRENCH and 9th Avenue Early in the Morning and took over to guard from 49 M.G. Coy. At 2 a.m. The Reserve Trench was heavily shelled & the trench was very much filled in. There was a marked absence of the Enemy's trench mortar. At 1 a.m. the gas alarm had risen and all troops stood to till 4-30 a.m. The usual artillery fire was carried out during the night 7/8 August.	
"	Aug 9th 1916		During the night 8/9 August the Enemy's M.G. fire was less than usual. At 2-45 p.m. on the 9th August a hostile Aeroplane came over our lines & dropped a bomb between our support & Reserve trench. We fired during the night. On the evening communication trench Drenched the day 9th August was quiet.	

WAR DIARY
or
INTELLIGENCE SUMMARY.
(Erase heading not required.)

Army Form C. 2118.

Place	Date	Hour	Summary of Events and Information	Remarks and references to Appendices
TRENCHES HULLUCH SECTION 1916.	Aug 10th		During the night 9/10 August the usual M.G. fire and sniping by the enemy went on. Indirect fire was carried out on the Main Street Hulluch and on communication trenches behind the enemy's lines during twilight. The day was very quiet probably owing to the misty weather rendering observation very difficult.	
"	Aug 11th		During the night 10/11 August the enemy's M.Gs and snipers were active. Indirect fire on roads, light railways, track and communication trenches. The enemy shelled our trenches at 3 p.m. and between 7 p.m. & 8 p.m.	

Army Form C. 2118.

WAR DIARY
or
INTELLIGENCE SUMMARY.
(Erase heading not required.)

Instructions regarding War Diaries and Intelligence Summaries are contained in F. S. Regs., Part II. and the Staff Manual respectively. Title pages will be prepared in manuscript.

Place	Date	Hour	Summary of Events and Information	Remarks and references to Appendices
TRENCHES HULLOCH SECTION	Aug 12th 1916.		During the night 11/12th August we fired on the main Street of HULLOCH crossroads behind the enemy's lines	
			The day was very quiet especially artillery	
		4pm	A hostile plane flew very high over our lines	
		7pm	A hostile plane dropped a bomb in front of our M.G. emplacement but it did not explode.	
"	Aug 13 1916.		The enemy's M.G.s & Snipers fire all night 12/13 August. Our M.G.s were also active	
			There was a heavy bombardment during the night in the direction of the DOUBLE CRASSIER.	
			The day was quiet.	

WAR DIARY or INTELLIGENCE SUMMARY

Army Form C. 2118.

(Erase heading not required.)

Place	Date	Hour	Summary of Events and Information	Remarks and references to Appendices
TRENCHES	14 Aug 1916		The night 13/14 August was very quiet and there was no incident of importance. Our M.Gs fired all night at selected targets. During the day there was a little shelling in this Reserve trench but no damage was done. At 11-15 pm gas was to have been discharged along the 16th Division front and part of the 8th Division front and a raid by the 9th Battn. Suffolks and 1st Munsters facilities but the wind was not favourable and operations were cancelled. M.Gs were however fired during the discharge of gas.	
"	15 Aug 1916		The usual indirect fire was carried out during the night. 14/15 August. After the discharge of Gas wards was cancelled at 12 noon an officer of the Company from the head of a sticker in the plain close to the village line carrying a German message which when translated gave information regarding one of Mr July. aeroplanes which was shot down on the night of 6th July.	

Army Form C. 2118.

WAR DIARY
or
INTELLIGENCE SUMMARY.
(Erase heading not required.)

Instructions regarding War Diaries and Intelligence Summaries are contained in F. S. Regs., Part II. and the Staff Manual respectively. Title pages will be prepared in manuscript.

Place	Date	Hour	Summary of Events and Information	Remarks and references to Appendices
TRENCHES HULLUCH SECTION	1916 16th Aug		Indirect M.G. fire was carried out during the night 15/16 August. The day was not particularly quiet with the exception of an explosion.	
"	17 August		The enemy's M.Gs. and Snipers were active during the night 16/17 August. Our M.Gs. fired continually all night on the enemy's communications. During the day the enemy's trench mortars were very active.	
"	18 August		During the night 17/18 August there was to have been a discharge of gas but the weather was unfavourable. Our M.Gs. fired during the day and night from covered emplacements on the enemy's communications. At 2 p.m. our artillery bombarded the enemy's trenches in the Hulluch Section doing considerable damage.	

T.2134. Wt. W708-776. 500000. 4/15. Sir J. C. & S.

Army Form C. 2118.

WAR DIARY
or
INTELLIGENCE SUMMARY.
(Erase heading not required.)

Instructions regarding War Diaries and Intelligence Summaries are contained in F. S. Regs., Part II. and the Staff Manual respectively. Title pages will be prepared in manuscript.

Place	Date	Hour	Summary of Events and Information	Remarks and references to Appendices
Trenches	19 August		Our M.G.s were active all the night 18/19 August. A little firing was done by day on roads behind the ridges in the GERMAN line. The day was very quiet.	
HULLUCH SECTION				
"	20th August		The night was very quiet with the exception of the enemy's M.G.s and snipers. Our M.G. fired continually all night. The enemy shelled the place in rear of the trenches periodically during the day with shrapnel. "19/20 August"	
"	21st August		During the night 20/21 August indirect fire was carried out on the enemy's back trenches and also fire of a special nature was carried out to down the morale of the enemy. If you wish took place. The day was fairly quiet. The enemy shelled out support and Reserve trench once or twice.	

Army Form C. 2118.

WAR DIARY
or
INTELLIGENCE SUMMARY.
(Erase heading not required.)

Instructions regarding War Diaries and Intelligence Summaries are contained in F. S. Regs., Part II. and the Staff Manual respectively. Title pages will be prepared in manuscript.

Place	Date	Hour	Summary of Events and Information	Remarks and references to Appendices
	1916			
[Cuinchy?]			The usual M.G. indirect fire was carried during the night	
TRENCHES	21/22nd August		Day was quiet. Germans were seen unloading	
HULLUCH SECTION			materials, packing cases from a wagon on the VERMIN-LES-[?] VIEIL ROAD.	
NOEUX-LES-MINES	22nd August		The Company was relieved, 6 guns in the RESERVE Trenches being taken over by 97 M.G. Company and the 5 guns in the village line by 24 M.G. Company. After the relief was complete the Company marched in 6 billets at NOEUX-LES-MINES arriving about 10 p.m.	
"	23rd August		The day was spent straightening the contents of the limbers and cleaning equipment	
LOZINGHEM	24th August	At 8-20 A.M.	The Company marched off from NOEUX-LES-MINES to LOZINGHEM where they went into billets arriving about 12-30 p.m.	

Army Form C. 2118.

WAR DIARY
or
INTELLIGENCE SUMMARY.
(Erase heading not required.)

Instructions regarding War Diaries and Intelligence Summaries are contained in F. S. Regs., Part II. and the Staff Manual respectively. Title pages will be prepared in manuscript.

Place	Date	Hour	Summary of Events and Information	Remarks and references to Appendices
LOZINGHEM.	26 August		The day was spent cleaning equipment & an inspection of rifles and the men went to the toilet	
LOZINGHEM.	27 August		The morning was spent preparing for G.O.C. 28th Infantry Brigade's inspection which took place at 3-30 p.m.	
LOZINGHEM.	28 August		Training in mechanism and cleaning of guns was done in the morning and preparing for the move on the following day in the afternoon.	
LOZINGHEM.	29 August		Company H.Q marched out at 11-15 a.m. to CHOQUES Station where they entrained for LONGEAU. Each section came on different trains at 3 hour interval.	
CORBIE	30 August		The Company marched from LONGEAU to CORBIE where they went in to billets for the night 30/31 August.	

WAR DIARY
or
INTELLIGENCE SUMMARY.

(Erase heading not required.)

Army Form C. 2118

Place	Date	Hour	Summary of Events and Information	Remarks and references to Appendices
	1916			
CORBIE	31 Aug.	10.45 a.m	The Company started on the march to the SANDPIT Camp near MÉAULTE arriving at about 4.45 p.m. Bivouacs were soon built and the Camp cleaned.	

M? Mucken Major
OC. 4D M.G. Company.

WAR DIARY

48th Machine Gun Company

FOR MONTH OF SEPTEMBER, 1916.

VOLUME

WAR DIARY
or
INTELLIGENCE SUMMARY.
(Erase heading not required.)

Army Form C. 2118.

Place	Date	Hour	Summary of Events and Information	Remarks and references to Appendices
SUZPT				
CAMP.				
	Sept 1st			
	Sept 2nd to Sept 5			
		6pm		
CARNEY	Sept 6th			

Army Form C. 2118.

WAR DIARY
or
INTELLIGENCE SUMMARY.
(Erase heading not required.)

Instructions regarding War Diaries and Intelligence Summaries are contained in F. S. Regs., Part II. and the Staff Manual respectively. Title pages will be prepared in manuscript.

Place	Date	Hour	Summary of Events and Information	Remarks and references to Appendices
NEW TAURAN	Apr 5	6pm	[illegible handwritten entries]	
"	Apr 6			

WAR DIARY
or
INTELLIGENCE SUMMARY.

Army Form C. 2118.

Place	Date	Hour	Summary of Events and Information	Remarks and references to Appendices
Hem The Bar	Sept 7th		Half Section were relieved by No. 2 RESERVE by half D Section Coy. Two days duty of A Section 1/Kings Liverpool Regt. were not relieved on this date during the day.	
"	Sept 8th		Nos. 4 Section in fire front line as relieved 1/7 & 2 M.G. Companies. Half D Section in Reserve Trench. B & C Section relieved 3 sections that had been out to L Gully Oz. 19-14. B & C Section were relieved by 5th & 6th Bn Dublin Fusiliers Infantry. At about 2 pm orders received that 1st RESERVE at GULLAEMENT were to move back to Bde HQ which are now situated on line from GULLY MOUNT STATION	
	2 pm			

WAR DIARY
or
INTELLIGENCE SUMMARY.
(Erase heading not required.)

Army Form C. 2118.

Instructions regarding War Diaries and Intelligence Summaries are contained in F. S. Regs., Part II. and the Staff Manual respectively. Title pages will be prepared in manuscript.

Place	Date	Hour	Summary of Events and Information	Remarks and references to Appendices
CORBIE	Sept 11th		The guns etc were cleaned and the men had a bath in the afternoon.	
CORBIE	Sept 12th		[illegible]	
"	Sept 17th		[illegible] ... buried in same	
"	Sept 18th	4/AM	The company fell in and marched to LA NEUVILLE to meet motor buses which conveyed them to MILLY arriving about 2-3 A.M. [illegible] went on to E. 17th Bge [illegible] LA PANNERIE	

Army Form C. 2118.

WAR DIARY
of
INTELLIGENCE SUMMARY.
(Erase heading not required.)

Place	Date	Hour	Summary of Events and Information	Remarks and references to Appendices
AILLY	Sept 20th		[illegible faded handwriting]	
		10.30	[illegible] LONG PRÉ [illegible]	
LONG PRÉ	Sept 21st	2.15 A.M.	The sister left LONG PRÉ and arrived at GODWAERSVELDE where the [illegible] entrained. They then marched to a billet [illegible] in a [illegible] about a mile East of WESTROUTRE.	

WAR DIARY
or
INTELLIGENCE SUMMARY.
(Erase heading not required.)

Army Form C. 2118.

Place	Date	Hour	Summary of Events and Information	Remarks and references to Appendices
CANADA CORNER	Sept 22nd		The Officers reconnoitred the trenches in the VIERSTRAAT SECTION and then prepared limbers for going to the parade & cleaned guns & ammunition.	
"	Sept 23		At 3 p.m. C & B Sections moved off and took up the guns positions in the VIERSTRAAT Section from the Yukon mot'n M.G. Coy.	
BRANDHOEK VIERSTRAAT SECTION	Sept 24		New gun position were reconnoitred and indirect worked out. The day was very quiet. Rye was a little trench mortar activity about 6 p.m.	
VIERSTRAAT SECTION	Sept 25th		Indirect fire was carried out during the night 24/25 Sept on the enemy's communication trenches. The day was very quiet. Enemy snipers were active at times.	

Army Form C. 2118.

WAR DIARY
or
INTELLIGENCE SUMMARY.
(Erase heading not required.)

Instructions regarding War Diaries and Intelligence Summaries are contained in F.S. Regs., Part II. and the Staff Manual respectively. Title pages will be prepared in manuscript.

Place	Date	Hour	Summary of Events and Information	Remarks and references to Appendices
VIERSTRAAT SECTION	Sept 26th		During the night Sept 25th/26th indirect fire on enemy's communication trenches and road junctions & troops used by enemy was carried out by Divl M.G.C. The day was as usual very quiet.	
"	Sept 27th		The company was relieved by 47 M.G. Coy with the exception 2 days. The guns which were relieved were relieved guns of 49 M.G. Coy. The 3 Brigades having been put in the line since the Brigade was shattered and moved further South.	
"	Sept 28th		The day was spent quietly. There was a little shelling in the support trench in the early hours of the morning and also behind the support trench between 2 and 3 p.m. The usual indirect fire by night was done by one M.G.	

Army Form C. 2118.

WAR DIARY
or
INTELLIGENCE SUMMARY.
(Erase heading not required.)

Place	Date	Hour	Summary of Events and Information	Remarks and references to Appendices
VIERSTAAT SECTION	Sept 29th		There was considerable trench mortar activity between 12.30 & 1-30 p.m. on both sides. The enemy fired a few rifle grenades also and one or two shrapnel shells during the rest of the day. It was quiet.	
"	Sept 30th		Volume of fire was carried out during the night 29/30 Sept in each and front brought to the enemy. It caused retaliation but not a little shelling during the day.	

McFletcher Captⁿ
O. C. 172 Company.

REPORT ON OPERATIONS
OF
48th INFANTRY BRIGADE
ON
9th and 10th September. 1916.
in
the attack on
GUINCHY.

To accompany War Diary.

1. PRELIMINARY DISPOSITIONS.

At 4.0 p.m. 7/9/16, 16th Division Operation Order No. 56 was received, and in accordance with these orders reliefs were carried out to put the Brigade in position for the assualt. On completion of the relief the Brigade was disposed as follows:-

7th IRISH RIFLES in LEFT SUBSECTION.
1st R. MUNSTER FUS. in RIGHT SUBSECTION.
9th R. DUBLIN FUSILIERS (SHERWOOD AND FAGAN TRENCHES).
8th R. DUBLIN FUSILIERS (Dummy Trench).
48th MACHINE GUN COMPANY.(MONTAUBAN).
156th FIELD COMPANY.R.E. (GUILLEMONT).

Orders were issued that as soon as the relief had been completed, work on assembly trenches for the assualt was to be proceeded with and two Companies of the HAMPSHIRE REGIMENT (PIONEERS) were detailed to assist the Battalions. Two lines of trenches were dug at T.20.a.1.3. and T.13.2.4.3., one behind the other, the second line to accomadate the Battalions carrying out the attack in the second phase. Great credit is due to all concerned that despite the tired state of all ranks, and constant shelling, trenches afforded good cover were made in the few available hours of the night of the 7th/8th and night of the 8th/9th September.1916. The willingness shewn by the rank and file in this trying and arduous work and their completing it by the time specified materially helped towards the success of the final objective.

2. 16th DIVISION OPERATION ORDER NO.57 was received at 10.40 a.m. 8/9/16 and 48th Infantry Brigade Operation Order No 64 was issued.
At 4 p.m. a conference of Officers commanding Battalions Machine Gun Company, and Light Trench Mortar Battery was held at which I explained my Operation Order and my intentions for the attack the next day. During the night 8th/9th September,1916, the 8th ROYAL DUBLIN FUSILIERS and 9th R. DUBLIN FUSILIERS moved up to positions of assembly in the trenches being specially dug, and the work on those trenches was carried on.
The Headquarters of all Battalions were moved into dugouts in trench T.19.@.5.0. and T.4.19.a.7.2.

3. On the morning of the 9th September,1916, the dispositions of the Battalions, Machine Gun Company, and Trench Mortar Battery for the assualt were as follows:-

In FRONT TRENCH with orders to take the FIRST OBJECTIVE and Consolidate it:-

| 7th ROYAL IRISH RIFLES. | 1st R. MUNSTER FUSILIERS. |
| 1 Section. T.M. Battery. | 1 Section T.M. Battery. |

-2-

In SUPPORT TRENCH with orders to take the SECOND OBJECTIVE and consolidate it:-

9th R. DUBLIN FUSILEERS.	8th R. DUBLIN FUSILIERS.
1. Section.M.G. COMPANY.	1 Section.M.G. COMPANY.
1 Section.156th COY.R.E.	1 Section 156th COY.R.E.

Five Guns of 48th MACHINE GUN COMPANY were disposed as follows:-

Two Guns GUILLEMONT STATION at S.24.d.8.9.
Two Guns about S.24.d.8.5.
One Gun about T.19.c.4.0.

Orders were issued to these guns to form a barrage on and behind FIRST OBJECTIVE during the bombardment, and to lift to a line 300 yards behind the SECOND OBJECTIVE at zero.

The remaining Stokes Guns of the 48th TRENCH MORTAR BATTERY, and Guns of the 48th MACHINE GUN COMPANY remained in reserve at QUARRY T.19.c.1½.3½.

Only two Stokes guns could be attached to the attacking force as the carrying up of ammunition for these guns monopolized the remainder of the personnel.

4. At 7.55 a.m. a message was received from the 7th Royal IRISH RIFLES stating that our Artillery was falling short, four shells bursting in our front line about T19.b.0.8. and at 8 a.m. a similar message was received from the 9th R.DUBLIN FUSILIERS. The 61st BRIGADE R.F.A. were warned by telephone, but at 8-45 a.m. and again at 10.30 a.m. messages were received from the 8th R. DUBLIN FUSILIERS asking for the barrage to be lifted, and the Left Group, Guards Division Artillery, were requested to take action in the matter. The 49th INFANTRY BRIGADE wired at 11.8 a.m. stating that the 8th R. INNISKILLING FUSILIERS reported our shells falling short in their trenches at T.19.b.0.3. to T.19.a.7.6.

5. At 10.5 a.m. I telephoned to 16th Division urging strongly that 8th R. INNISKILLING FUSILIERS (who were in rear of the right Battalions) should advance in close support of 8th R. DUBLIN FUSILIERS as this would strengthen the centre of the Divisional Front at the junction between the 47th and 48th Brigades, and where it was essential that there should be no check. The 16th Division approved this by telephone and confirmed it by message (G.88) Orders were accordingly issued to 8th R. INNISKILLING FUSILIERS under No B.M.B.869 to advance in close support of the 8th R. DUBLIN FUSILIERS and to assist in the consolidation of the SECOND OBJECTIVE when gained.

6. Message No.G.89 was received from 16th Division at 1.15p.m. stating that the patrols ordered in para.9 of Operation Orders woulo only be sent out by 3rd GUARDS BRIGADE on completion of relief.

7. O.C. 7th ROYAL IRISH RIFLES reported by telephone at 2.p.m that he then had only 150 rifles available for the attack. The 16th Division were immediately informed that it was imperative that another Battalion of the 49th Infantry Brigade should be placed at my disposal, and at 2.20 p.m. a message (g.96) was received, sanctioning this course.

At 2.45 p.m. the 49th Infantry Brigade wired (B.M.C.871) that the 7th R. IRISH FUSILIERS would come under the orders of the G.O.C. 48th INFANTRY BRIGADE forthwith, this Battalion was instructed by wire (B.M.B.878) to get in touch with O.C. 7th R. IRISH RIFLES at T.19.b.7.3. and to support that Battn. in its advance so timing it to move forward in rear of the barrage at zero hour. This movement was well carried out and great credit is due to the Officer Commanding who had little time to issue necessary orders.

8. In view of the fact that no reserves were now available a(XXXXXXXX) telephone message was sent to 16th Division requesting that a battalion of the Guards should be pushed up to BERNAFAY WOOD without delay.

9. The ORDER OF BATTLE WAS now as follows:-

For FIRST OBJECTIVE.

LEFT SUB-SECTION.	RIGHT SUB-SECTION.
7th R. IRISH RIFLES.	1st R. MUNSTER FUSILIERS.
7th R. IRISH FUSILIERS. (49th Inf. Bde.,)	1 Sectn. T.M. Battery.
1 Sectn. T.M. BATTERY.	

For SECOND OBJECTIVE.

8th R. DUBLIN FUSILIERS.	8th R. DUBLIN FUSILIERS.
1 Sectn. 156 Field COY.R.E.	8th R. INNISKILLING FUS., (49th Inf. Bde.,)
	1 Sectn. 156 FIELD COY.R.E.

Five Guns 48th MACHINE GUN COMPANY disposed as follows:-

Two at GUILLEMONT STATION S.34.d.8.9.
Two at about S.24.d.8.5.
One at about T.19.c.4.6.

Remaining Guns of 48th M.G. COMPANY and 48th T.M. BATTERY being in Reserve at QUARRY T.19.c.1½.3½.

Headquarters. 156 FIELD COY.R.E. in GUILLEMONT.

10. THE ASSUALT.

At zero (4.45 p.m.) the line advanced under the artillery barrage on the FIRST OBJECTIVE, each Battalion assualting with four Companies in the front line, on a front of one Platoon per Company, Platoons at 40 yards distance.

FIRSTPHASE.

RIGHT BATTALION (1st R.MUNSTER FUSILIERS). At the outset very heavy Officer casualties were suffered, and the Second in Command, who was leading the assualt was killed within fifty yards of the FIRST OBJECTIVE.

The RIGHT COMPANY experienced considerable opposition on their right flank, due to the fact that the 8th R. MUNSTER FUSILIERS on our right (47th Inf.Bde) was checked with apparently heavy loss by a Machine Gun about T.20.a.½.8. The Officer Commanding this Company therefore wheeled to the right and occupied a position in the German Trench- T.20.a.1.3½. to T.20.c.½.7. - where he dug himself in.

The second Company from the right, commanded by the Company-Sergeant-Major, observing that the right was held up wheeled and charged the enemy, driving them out of their position. A German Officer re-organised his men, and occupied a trench further to the east, but they were out-flanked on the west and northwest and dispersed with heavy losses.

Owing to the absence of Officers, the third and fourth Companies from the right lost direction somewhat and were eventually merged with other Units. They were carried beyond the FIRST OBJECTIVE, and it was not until the arrival of the O.C. 8th R. DUBLIN FUSILIERS that men were recalled and put to the task of consolidating the line of the FIRST OBJECTIVE.

The Stokes Gun attached to this Battalion(XXXXXXX) did not come into action here as the Officer in charge had been killed, and the gun team separated from their ammunition carrying party. The Officer in charge of the left gun noticing that the team on the right were disorganised, ran and collected as amnt men and as much ammunition as he could XXXX, attaching the remnants to the left team, the action of which will be described later.

The 8th R. DUBLIN FUSILIERS supported by the 8th R. INNISKILLING FUS(, XXXXXXXXXXXXXX) followed by the 1st .R.MUNSTER FUSILIERS at 100 yards distance in the first phase of the attack,

FIRST PHASE.

LEFT BATTALION. The 7th R. IRISH RIFLES closely followed by the 7th R.IRISH FUSILIERS advanced at zero hour under the artillery barrage and reached the FIRST OBJECTIVE about 4.57 p.m. meeting with but slight resistance and suffering slight casualties.

The amalgamated Stokes Gun Team mentioned above arrived at the first objective about the same time as the Infantry, and a party of the enemy (about 40 men under an offider) offering a stout resistance to the second advance, the Stokes Guns were withdrawn to shell holes a little in the rear of our line, from which fire was opened on the enemy, who, after about twenty rounds had been dropped around them promptly surrendered.

After this incident the range was increased and a barrage created which assisted the second assualting force in their advance.

12. ## SECOND PHASE.

RIGHT. The 8th R. DUBLIN FUSILIERS advanced to the SECOND OBJECTIVE at zero, plus 40 minutes (5.25 p.m.) and gained the position without encoutering very serious opposition. At 5.40 p.m. it was found that the Battalion had proceeded about 300 yards beyond the objective, and the Commanding Officer took prompt speps to bring back his men who had by now been reinforced by the 8th VR.INNISKILLING FUS. to the real objective, and to start them on digging a trench about 50 yards east of the German trench.

At this time a number of troops were seen on the road running due east from GUINCHY, whom it was at first thought belonged to the Brigade on our right. The light being bad it was difficult to distinguish who they were - a Vickers Gun was therefore placed in position to watch this road.

The construction of the Strong Point 42 was now proceeded with and two Lewis Guns were placed at this Point with orders to carefully watch their left flank, which at this time appeared to be unprotected. This strong point was of immense value and enabled us to beat two counter attacks - the first at 11 p.m. 9.9.16, when the enemy came forward with a Machine Gun and the second at 4.0 a.m. 10.9.16 when the enemy tried to work in between the two roads running through T.14.a.

In the meantime some of the 7th R. IRISH FUSILIERS who had been on by the 9th R. DUBLIN FUSILIERS moved towards Point 42, where, on their arrival, the O.C. 8th Royal Dublin Fusiliers allotted them the task of consolidating the line between his left and the 9th R. DUBLIN FUSILIERS' right, where there was a small gap.

A Vickers Gun was placed in position in the cnetre of GINCHY T.14.c$\frac{1}{2}$.7. to enfilade the wood on the east of the village
About 7.0 p.m. an aeroplane passed over our position

at T.13.b.2.2. diving suddenly to drop a message. This message was picked up by an N.C.O. of the 8th R. Dublin Fusilers, and it was found to contain a map showing the positions of ourtroops sketched in blue chalk, alsoaa note to the effect that all was proceeding well along the whole line. The information given was invaluable and helped to clear up the situation at various points

During this time the consolidation of the position was proceeded with, with good results despite constant shelling and machine gun fire, and small patrols were sent out to get in touch with the Briagde on our right, but it was found that they had not advanced to the position allotted to them, and it was not until 10.0 a.m.on the 10.9.16 that touch was effected with the GRENADIER-GUARDS, who had relieved the 47th Infantry Brigade on our right during the night.

About 10.0 p.m. it was reportedto Battalion Headquarts that our troops were-retiring from the second objective. The Commanding Officer rallied the men, who consisted of some sixty or seventy of all Units, and led them back to where they had to dig.

SECOND PHASE.
LEFT. The 9th R. DUBLIN FUSILIERS passed through the FIRST OBJECTIVE at 5.25 p.m. on to he SECOND OBJECTIVE carrying with them some of the 7th R. IRISH RIFLES and 7th R. IRISH FUSILIERS, the latter inclining towards Point 42. as described above, where they filled in the gap between the right and left Battalions.

The line of the SECOND OBJECTIVE was not easy to distinguish, and the attack went beyond it. This mistake was recognised by a sublatern officer of the 7th R. IRISH RIFLES who then brought his own men and men of the 9th R.DUBLIN FUSILIERS back to the correct line, and proceeded to consolidate it.

The section of the 156 FIELD COY.R.E. proceeded to Strong Point 40, where the work was put in ahnd at once , but it was soon discovered at once that the 55th Division on our left had not come up, and that our flank was therefore expoded .

At this junature the Officer Commanding the 8th ROYAL DUBLIN FUSILIERS arrived at Headquarters,7th R. IRISH RIFLES to consult with the O.CM who had been knocked over by a shell and severely shaken. At the request of the O.CM.07th ROYAL IRISH RIFLES the O.C. 8th R. DUBLIN FUSILIERS made a tour of the wholeBrigade front, and withdrew same parties of the 7th ROYAL IRISH RIFLES from the SECOND OBJECTIVE to consolidate the first objective and extended the 9th R.DUBLIN FUSILIERS from about T.13. central to the GINCHY-FLERS ROAD so as to make connection with the 8th R.DUBLIN FUSILIERS.

The Section of the 156 FIELD COMPANYR.E. had in the meantime withdrawn to T.13.central where a strong point was made with One Vickers Gun and three Lewis Guns - the line now being consolidated running from T.13.b.8.5. Section assumed control of this position and rendered valuable service in capably dealing with a situation which was throughout a difficult one...

On reaching the SECOND OBJECTIVE It was found that the 55th Division had not come up on the left, the artillery were requested to lengthen the barrage north-westwards in order to cover Point 42 and on our left flank.

A Vickers gun was placed in position to enfilade the GINCHY-FLERS ROAD and another was put in position the most northerly point of GINCHY WOOD.

Touch with the troops on our left was eventually established by bombing posts and patrols sent out from T.13 central.

12.
In all it is estimated that 200 unwounded prisoners were taken by the Brigade.

13.
The sequence of events were as follows:

5.7 p.m. Telephone message from 16th Division: "Corps report that First Objective in GINCHY has been gained". Information received by wireless from aeroplane.

5.12 p.m. 74th Brigade R.F.A. report "Infantry got GINCHY" (Aeroplane report gives the time of taking GINCHY as 6.47 p.m. which is more likely correct).

5.13 p.m. 75th Brigade R.F.A. reported "One yellow flare seen at T.19.b.3.9."
F.O.O. reports our Infantry advancing on left with slight opposition.
Infantry held up on right by heavy shelling.

5.15 p.m. 47th Inf Brigade reported that they had gained their first objective.
(which was afterwards found to be incorrect).

5.23 p.m. 61st Brigade R.F.A. reported "Infantry meeting with great opposition at T.19.b.2.9.

5.5.50 p.m. 75th Brigade.R.F.A. F.O.O. reported timed 5.45 p.m. "Enemy shelling GINCHY-GUILLEMONT ROAD and GUILLEMONT-LONGUEVAL Road heavily with 8 inch" Also that at 5.18 p.m. Infantry seen on South edge of GINCHY -T.19.b.3.9. - T.19.b.8.9.
(This latter was confirmed by aeroplane observer)

6.8 p.m. F.O.O. Guards Division Artillery reported, timed 5.40 p.m. Infantry have reached right hand side of Ginchy with heavy opposition. They seem to have reached T.14.c.9.1. to T.13.central. Infantry on right are still meeting with heavy opposition. Parties of our own Infantry seen retiring from left side of GINCHY (Query wounded or prisoners). Enemy's fire very intense"

6.10 p.m. 7th R. INNISKILLING Fusiliers reported: "GINCHY taken"

6.18 p.m. Guards Division Artillery reported "Aeroplane reports final objective gained "on right and left - centre held up by Germans at T.20.a.central

-8-.

 6.20 p.m. 16th Division reported "47th Infantry Brigade held up at T.20.a.centra."

 6.36 p.m. "Guards Division Artillery reported:"Infantry "seem to have done well on the line-T.14.c.5.4. "to T.14.%.9.5. In front of attcak on-right "hand of GINCHY, Infantry met with much opposition "Enemy have now renewed barrage along line "T.qr.c.8.5. - T.20.b.3.0.

 6.55 p.m. Guards Division Artillery reported: "55th Division held up in HAY ALLEY. "Situation not clear.

 7.20 p.m. 7th R. Irish Rifles reported that both objectives were taken by 6.20 p.m. and that the lines were being consolidated, Casualties very severe.

14. On reports coming in that heavy casualties had been incurred amongst all ranks, and that no Officers at all were left in the 9th R. DUBLIN FUSILIERS(this proved incorrect as two junior subalterns came out with the Battalion) a telephone was sent to the 16th Division asking for a Battalion of the Guards to be sent up at once as it was necessary to reinforce the line and at 7.40 p.m. a message was received from 16th Division stating that a Battalion of Guards would take over the line running east from GINCHY at T.14.c.Central.

15. At about 11.30 p.m. two Companies of the WELSH GUARDS arrived at the Headquarters 7th R. IRISH RIFLES and one Company took over the line held by the Battalion. The 7th R. IRISH RIFLES then withdrew to BERNAFAY WOOD, where soup, etc., was in readiness for the men and then marched to CARNOY. It was not until 1.30 a.m. 10.9.16 that the remainder of the WELSH GUARDS reported to O.C. 8th R.DUBLIN FUSILIERS and stated that they order to relieve from Point 42. to T.13.central only. Their left Company was placed in position, relieving part of the 9.th R. DUBLIN FUSILIERS. During this operation 14 of the enemy who were within our lines surrendered. The remainder of the Battalion was relieved by the GRENADIER GUARDS late on the morning of the 10.9.16, the relief on the right of the line only being commenced at 9.45 a.m. Relief was completed at 11 a.m. and the 8th R. DUBLIN FUSILIERS then proceeded to TRONNS WOOD across country - the GINCHY -GUILLEMONT Road being heavily shelled at the time by the enemy.

Field Kitchens of all Units were brought to BERNAFAY WOOD, and a meal provided for the men before they continued their march to Reservepppositions.

16. GENERAL REMARKS.
During the preliminary bombardment by our artillery several shells fell in our own trenches, unfortunately causing many casualties, but, during the attack, and

causing many casualties, but, during the attack and subsequently the work of the artillery was excellent and could not have been better. The barrage was lifted with regularity and in strict accordance with the programme, and on our reaching the final objective the curtain of fire was maintained at my request for some considerable time with splended effect.

Telephone communication between Brigade H.Q. and the four Battalions was effected through the Brigade Report Centre, which was establishes in QUARRY, GUILLEMONT, at T.19.c.1½.4. and it was entirely to this system that the moving up of the 7th R. IRISH FUSILIERS just before the attack was amde possible.

17. Lines were frequently cut, but on the whole communication was amintained with extraordinary success and great crefit id due to the Linesman who were constantly out repairing the lines ander very heavt fire.

Arrangements were made for Visual Signalling but owing to the smoke from barrage messages could not be read.

18. It is with great regret that I have to report the Brigade suffered very severe casualties prior to, and in, the attack. The figures as at present known are:

OFFICERS.		OTHER RANKS.	
Killed	21.	Killed	170.
Wounded	56.	Wounded	858.
Missing	5.	Missing	296.
Total.	82.	Total	1324.

These figures include the following Specialists:
Signallers.......48.
Lewis Gunners...131.

19. CONCLUSION.

In conclusion I wish to express my extreme satisfaction at the spirit, courage, and determination displayed by all ranks during the operations and in particular of the action od Lieut-Col., E. BELLINGHAM, 8th R. DUBLIN FUSILIERS, who at atime when troops were elated with success and without Officers was able to control the situation and organise the defences. When it is remembered that the troops had been out in the so-called trenches which were in reality merely shell holes, for five days and night prior to the attack, during which period they were wet through by rain and did not have the chance of obtaining a hot meal, I submit that the highest credit is reflected on all ranks that the capture of GINCHY was effected under these adverse conditions, and that the traditions of the Irish race were worthily upheld by these men of the New ARmies.

I have already submitted the names of Officers, N.C.O's and Men who showed marked ability and courage for immediate award, and I shall have the honour to submit names of others whose actions only just fell short of the highest standard for recognition in due course.

(Signed). F. RAMSAY.
Brigadier General.
Commanding. 48th Infantry Brigade.

15.9.16.

WAR DIARY

MONTH OF OCTOBER, 1916.

VOLUME

48th Machine Gun Company

WAR DIARY
INTELLIGENCE SUMMARY

October 1916   48 Machine Gun Company   Army Form C. 2118.

Place	Date	Hour	Summary of Events and Information	Remarks and references to Appendices
VIERSTRAAT SECTION	Oct 1st 1916		During the night Sept 30/Oct 1st Indirect fire was carried at by our guns on the enemy's communications. The troops stood to more of the right on account of a suspected attack by the enemy. There was a little trench mortar activity during the day.	
"	Oct 2nd 1916.		The enemy's Snipers and M.g.s were not so active during the night 1st/2nd Oct at Khal. Our M.g.s did the usual indirect fire. The day was exceptionally quiet probably owing to the bad weather.	
"	Oct 3rd 1916		During the same our M.g.s were firing the indirect fire at night the enemy's M.gs did not fire, but they opened later when our guns had ceased. The weather was bad again & the day quiet.	
"	Oct 4th		The enemy were a little more active during the day. trench with little trench mortars and artillery. The usual M.g. fire & sniping went on throughout the night.	

Army Form C. 2118.

WAR DIARY
or
INTELLIGENCE SUMMARY.
(Erase heading not required.)

Instructions regarding War Diaries and Intelligence Summaries are contained in F. S. Regs., Part II. and the Staff Manual respectively. Title pages will be prepared in manuscript.

Place	Date	Hour	Summary of Events and Information	Remarks and references to Appendices
VIERSTRAAT SECTION.	5th Oct. 1916.		The morning was spent in firing, riding instructions & to the two SECTIONS out of the line. The Guns and Ammunition were cleaned and the Machine Gunners attended stables at the usual time. Box Respirator drill and fitting clothing were carried out in the afternoon. The day was quiet in the line.	
"	Oct. 6th. 1916.		The Officer Commanding the Company Major N.V.BLACKER went on leave to England and Lieut. P.D.MULHOLLAND took charge in his absence. Owing to unfavourable weather very little was done by the Sections in Reserve. All was quiet in the line.	
"	Oct. 7th. 1916.		Fine weather prevailed. Instruction in Machine Gunnery for the attached men was carried on and Riding classes were continued. In the afternoon fitting & testing of box respirators at the Divisional Gas School was carried out. The whole Company is now complete with Box Respirators.	
"	Oct. 8th. 1916.		The weather was bad. Instruction in Machine Gunnery was carried on in the building of the stables proceeded satisfactorily, the roofing was finished by the evening. In the afternoon the G.O.C. inspected the Rear Guns, all was satisfactory. No indirect fire was carried out, in the night, owing to a heavy SE wind and rocking forts being out.	
"	Oct. 9th. 1916.		The sections were relieved. This was completed by 1 P.M., a new Gun Position located by the G.O.C. was occupied and improved on it were started.	

Army Form C. 2118.

WAR DIARY
or
INTELLIGENCE SUMMARY.
(Erase heading not required.)

Instructions regarding War Diaries and Intelligence Summaries are contained in F.S. Regs., Part II. and the Staff Manual respectively. Title pages will be prepared in manuscript.

Place	Date	Hour	Summary of Events and Information	Remarks and references to Appendices
VIERSTRAAT SECTION	10th Oct. 1916.		The building of the stables progressed favourably. The line was quiet throughout the day with the exception of one shell which wounded two men of this Company. Sgt. Duckworth and Pte. Harrison. We have been unable to carry out any rocket fire party as there have been numerous wiring parties out.	
"	11th Oct. 1916.		The two Sections in reserve were overhauling and cleaning limbers. Belt boxes arrived from Railhead and the company is now complete in Belts & Belt boxes. The G.O.C. Division was to have inspected the wagon lines but failed to do so. Everything has been quiet on the line with exception of slight trench Mortar activity.	
"	12th Oct. 1916.		Instruction in riding for the M. Gunners was continued today. C. & D. sections are improving rapidly at Box Respirator Drill. The reserve sections were paraded today. The line was very quiet.	
"	13th Oct. 1916.		The relief between the left and right half Companies took place this morning. The half company resting in billets had baths this afternoon. The line has been very quiet all day.	
"	14th Oct. 1916.		Indirect fire was carried out entirely on one enemy C.T. and a crossroad. Hostile artillery became active today for the first time since we have occupied this sector. There was an organised Trench Mortar bombardment of the enemy's line this afternoon. A broken bogie of a G.S. wagon was found and brought to the horse lines today.	

Army Form C. 2118.

WAR DIARY
or
INTELLIGENCE SUMMARY.
(Erase heading not required.)

Instructions regarding War Diaries and Intelligence Summaries are contained in F.S. Regs., Part II. and the Staff Manual respectively. Title pages will be prepared in manuscript.

Place	Date	Hour	Summary of Events and Information	Remarks and references to Appendices
VIERSTRAAT Section.	15th Oct. 1916.		The reserve section attended Church parade and carried out Box Respirator drill in the afternoon. An advance party was carried out last night on German C.T. running East from pt. N.20.6.94. Section X. reported at O.2.oc.2.8. German artillery periodically shelled the neighbourhood of Sec. Gun position.	
"	16th Oct		The usual indirect fire was carried out during the night 15/16 October. During the day the enemy shelled the left of "C" Brigade line but did no damage. There was some trench mortar activity.	
"	17th Oct		The enemy was fairly active with their M.G.s & Snipers during the night 16/17 October. He did indirect fire on his communications during the day on their right. "A" Section relieved "C" Section and "B" Section relieved "D" at about 11-30 A.M. "C" & "D" Section withdrew to Bny H.Q.	

2353 Wt. W2544/1454 700,000 5/15 D. D. & L. A.D.S.S./Forms/C. 2118.

Army Form C. 2118.

WAR DIARY
or
INTELLIGENCE SUMMARY.
(Erase heading not required.)

Instructions regarding War Diaries and Intelligence Summaries are contained in F.S. Regs., Part II. and the Staff Manual respectively. Title pages will be prepared in manuscript.

Place	Date	Hour	Summary of Events and Information	Remarks and references to Appendices
VIERSTRAAT SECTION	18th Oct		The enemy was quiet during the day and during the night 17/18 Oct their M.Gs and Snipers were active. Our M.Gs &c did the usual indirect fire during the night.	
VIERSTRAAT SECTION	19th Oct.		Inclement weather greatly interfered with the works in hand. The enemy was quiet during the day with the exception of some spasmodic Trench Mortar activity. Machine Guns & Snipers were fairly active during the night. The usual indirect fire from our Machine Guns was carried out during the night.	
VIERSTRAAT SECTION	20th Oct:		2/Lieut. Edwards joined the Company yesterday & was posted to A Section. The enemy displayed machine gun activity at one of our planes. Also shrapnel. An enemy plane was observed over our lines & was bombarded by our anti-aircraft guns. No result was apparent. A certain amount of Artillery activity was noticed by our front guns without eliciting much reply. The usual indirect fire was carried out by our guns at night.	
VIERSTRAAT SECTION	21st Oct:		The Sections were relieved to-day. Day & night quiet on our front excepting usual enemy activity with rifles at night. The usual indirect fire was carried out by our guns.	

Army Form C. 2118.

WAR DIARY
or
INTELLIGENCE SUMMARY.
(Erase heading not required.)

Instructions regarding War Diaries and Intelligence Summaries are contained in F. S. Regs., Part II. and the Staff Manual respectively. Title pages will be prepared in manuscript.

Place	Date	Hour	Summary of Events and Information	Remarks and references to Appendices
VIERSTRAAT Section	22nd Oct.		Night quiet. During the day 7 light shells fell near our gun emplacement at GOETHALS FARM. Usual M. G's & Snipers at night. Indirect fire was carried out during the night.	
VIERSTRAAT Section	23rd Oct.		Usual hostile M.G's & Snipers at night. Otherwise quiet. During the morning & evening sweeping fire was carried out attacking the M.G's & Snipers.	
VIERSTRAAT Section	24th Oct.		Quiet day & night, with exception of usual M.G's Snipers. Indirect fire was carried out during the night by both I.F. guns. The usual work in Rams was continued.	
VIERSTRAAT Section	25th Oct.		The day & night passed quietly. Enemy M.G's Snipers as usual. The usual 2nd rect fire has been carried out during the night. Relief took place today.	
VIERSTRAAT Section	26th Oct.		The day & night passed quietly. Indirect fire was carried out both during the night as usual. There is nothing of importance to report.	
VIERSTRAAT Section	27th Oct.		The day & night passed quietly. Indirect fire carried out as usual. Nothing else of importance to report.	
VIERSTRAAT Section	28th Oct.		Day & night quiet. Portion of Vta Gelder Rawing to S' Portion was blown in during the afternoon but is now being cleared. Usual Indirect fire carried out.	
VIERSTRAAT Section	29th Oct.		Day & night quiet. The usual Indirect fire was carried out by our guns. Preparations for the Raid were completed. Otherwise nothing special to report.	
VIERSTRAAT Section	30th Oct.		The raid was carried out but so far no details to hand. Our guns cooperated. 4 guns on the actual raid, four guns on dummy. No casualties to the Company. Work on various positions proceeded with	

Army Form C. 2118.

WAR DIARY
or
INTELLIGENCE SUMMARY.

(Erase heading not required.)

Place	Date	Hour	Summary of Events and Information	Remarks and references to Appendices
VIERSTRAAT Section	Oct 31		The day & night have been quiet. During the day some left M.G. shells fell near our R.A. position & one pinnacle holes have been blown. Direct hit was carried out by our gun at 1.52 position. Works as usual.	
VIERSTRAAT Section	Nov 1		Day + night quiet. The usual work was carried out on Emplacements, Dug Outs, Indirect lines + cover up communication trenches. In taking over emplacements at S.P. 113 from 49 h. G. Coy.	

Chaney Capt.
O.C. 48 M.G. Coy.

WAR DIARY.

FOR

MONTH OF NOVEMBER, 1916.

VOLUME 8

48th Machine Gun Company.

Army Form C. 2118.

WAR DIARY
or
INTELLIGENCE SUMMARY.

(Erase heading not required.)

WAR DIARY

No 48 Company Machine Gun Corps

from

1st November 1916.

to

30th November 1916.

Chisholm Capt.
O.C. No 48 Coy. M.G. Corps.

Vol. 8.

Army Form C. 2118.

WAR DIARY
or
INTELLIGENCE SUMMARY.
(Erase heading not required.)

Instructions regarding War Diaries and Intelligence Summaries are contained in F. S. Regs., Part II. and the Staff Manual respectively. Title pages will be prepared in manuscript.

Place	Date	Hour	Summary of Events and Information	Remarks and references to Appendices
	1.11.16.		The day & night were quiet. Indirect fire was carried out as usual. We took over positions held by 49 W.G Coy at S.P.11.a. Otherwise nothing.	
	2.11.16.		Nothing to report. Usual Indirect fire during the night. Relief took place during the day	
	3.11.16.		Nothing to report. Indirect fire as usual. Work commenced on emplacement at FORT CALGARY. Trench mortar activity in region of S.A position.	
	4.11.16.		His Royal Highness the Duke of Connaught passed through during day. Indirect fire to Harval trench up to battery of MITTZ fired by us between 3 pm & 5.30 pm and down retaliating pretty heavily.	
	5.11.16.		Evening the report - hand indirect fire during night - with an enemy. This time was spent in filling sand-bags for Relief and work on bullies is being proposed with. Day quiet.	
	6.11.16.		Relief took place today — many casualties by 11 A.M. My bn. many very great. Nothing to report.	

Army Form C. 2118.

WAR DIARY
or
INTELLIGENCE SUMMARY.
(Erase heading not required.)

Place	Date	Hour	Summary of Events and Information	Remarks and references to Appendices
	7/11/16		Some retaliation from enemy in consequence of raid by 4/Sqdn. But little enemy arty. direct retaliation. I. Quiet - fire was carried out. Eny N 24 S.6.6. The arty direct repeat hostile - repairing damage done by heavy rain fell otherwise nothing to report	
	8/11/16		Enemy machine guns active, replying vigorously to our bursts of fire. Hostile trenches which were manned at being dug fell in S.P. 11A and P's 3 & 4. The digging being hindered by our guns. The day was very quiet.	
	9/11/16		Indirect fire was carried out back of railway in Petite - Bois also communication trenches and to the C.unit.f of NY.S.C. HAETE WOOD through N 24 S88. Repairs to S1 and S2 continued. Construction of ammunition shelter at R.I and R.2 front out. bringt.	
VIERSTRAAT SECTOR.	10th Nov 1916.		Indirect fire was carried out last night from I.F.3 and I.F.4 . 2000 rounds being expended. There was no hostile activity of any importance with the exception of aircraft activity no doubt numerous photographs have been taken of our Trench system today. The relief of the two sections in the line was carried out today.	
	11/11/16		The indirect fire was carried out as usual from I.F.3 & I.F.4 . 2500 rounds being expended. There was no hostile activity - the day might - being very quiet. Work on the new emplacement at 10 P. which may with S.T. 11.A. is being continued	

Army Form C. 2118.

WAR DIARY
or
INTELLIGENCE SUMMARY.
(Erase heading not required.)

Instructions regarding War Diaries and Intelligence Summaries are contained in F. S. Regs., Part II. and the Staff Manual respectively. Title pages will be prepared in manuscript.

Place	Date	Hour	Summary of Events and Information	Remarks and references to Appendices
VIERSTRAAT SECTION.	12th Nov. 1916.		Capt. Connell A.D.C. ii. visited the Trenches for G.S.O.1. To see the M.G. Emplacements and collect information. A certain amount of Enemy Trench Mortar activity between 3 and 4 P.M. Today. Lieut. Roberts arrived today to take over command of the Company from Capt. Cadiz. A great deal of work is being carried out with a view to improving the conditions on the farm. (KLONDYKE FARM.)	
''	13th Nov. 1916.		No hostile activity today. Indirect fire was carried out last night, 4000 rounds were fired. Work on the farm is being continued.	
''	14th Nov. 1916.		Lieut Roberts officially took over command of the Company and Capt Cadiz returned to his original Company. The line has been very quiet today. The enemy sent over a few shrapnel shells towards KEMMEL HILL to the afternoon. Indirect fire was carried out last night. 5500 rounds were fired.	
''	15th Nov. 1916.		Indirect fire was carried out last night by the guns. 9,250 rounds were fired. PETIT BOIS having a particularly large amount of attention being paid to it. An air duel was fought today just above YORK HOUSE and it appeared that the German plane appeared in difficulties having on hover landing in its own territory.	
''	16th Nov. 16		Indirect fire was carried out last night by the guns. 9000 rounds were fired. The Church in WYTSCHAETE and the surrounding ground received punishment. The day has been quiet and very cold.	

Army Form C. 2118.

WAR DIARY
or
INTELLIGENCE SUMMARY.
(Erase heading not required.)

Instructions regarding War Diaries and Intelligence Summaries are contained in F. S. Regs., Part II. and the Staff Manual respectively. Title pages will be prepared in manuscript.

Place	Date	Hour	Summary of Events and Information	Remarks and references to Appendices
VIERSTRAAT SECTION	17 Nov 1916		Indirect fire was carried out last night. 2500 rounds were fired by the guns. The 36th Inst. Bun on Convalescent attack on our right lasting 1hr. The day passed very quietly.	
"	18 Nov 1916		Indirect fire was carried out last night. 4500 rounds were fire by the guns. The weather was changed for the worse, Rain in nearly the whole of the day. "A" and "B" sections were relieved by "3" and "C" section respectively this morning.	
	19 Nov 1916		Indirect fire was carried out last night. 3750 rounds were fired. "C" section stood to form 1.30 A.M — 3.30 A.M. the morning as the gas alarm was sounded on the right of the centre sector, there was unusual T.M. and Whirig-bang activity on our right chiefly. The day has been dull and moderately cold. The G.O.C. Bde returned from PARIS today, he however did not come here.	
	20 Nov 1916		Indirect fire was carried out last night. 2750 rounds were fired by the guns. The day has passed very quietly. A great amount of work has been carried out with a view to improve its conditions in billets.	
	21 Nov 1916		Indirect fire was carried out last night. 2800 rounds were fired by 2 guns. Day has been very quiet. Work is still progressing on the improvement of billets.	
	22 Nov /16		Indirect fire was carried out last night. 2850 rds were fired. 2 Guns took on dugout emplacement is proceeding very well. The dugtons have quick	

WAR DIARY
or
INTELLIGENCE SUMMARY.
(Erase heading not required.)

Army Form C. 2118.

Place	Date	Hour	Summary of Events and Information	Remarks and references to Appendices
VIERSTRAAT SECTION	23 Nov 1916.		Indirect fire was carried out last night. 12,100 rounds were fired. The enemy retaliated its afternoon in the direction of GOET HALS FARM with small shells. No damage was done. The rest billets are properly satisfactory though the farmer owning the farm is putting many difficulties in our way. The day has been cold and dull. There was slight T.M. activity on the night of S.I. position.	
"	24 Nov 1916.		Indirect fire was carried out last night. 3600 rounds were fired. Our artillery completely quieted all enemy "Rum Jar" activity in afternoon at 3.P.M. The nunnery of the nut-bullet became very obnoxious this morning and senior L.P's were very nearly resorted to, however the differents were arranged satisfactorily to both parties. The day has been very cloudy and military.	
"	25 Nov 1916.		Indirect fire was carried out last night. 3250 rounds were fired. The day has been extremely wet and depressing.	
"	26 Nov 1916.		Indirect fire was carried out last night. 3,100 rounds were fired. A and B Section relieved C and D Sections this morning. The weather has improved today.	
"	27 Nov 1916.		Indirect fire was carried out last night. 7750 rounds were fired. Enemy air craft were very active about mid-day today though in far as could be ascertained no aeroplanes were brought down. The day has been quite warm and sunny.	
"	28 Nov 1916.		Indirect fire was carried out last night. 6250 Rounds were fired. Operation orders for a DUMMY RAID are attached. The day has been cold and towards the evening a very heavy damp mist came down.	I

Army Form C. 2118.

WAR DIARY
or
INTELLIGENCE SUMMARY.
(Erase heading not required.)

Place	Date	Hour	Summary of Events and Information	Remarks and references to Appendices
VIGNACOURT Section	29 Nov 1916.		The day has been very quiet. Two o'clock it was fired similar to last night. Operations of yesterday's show are postponed. It has been very cold and damp today.	
	30 Nov 1916.		Indirect fire was carried out last night. 2760 rounds were fired. The day has been very cold. A heavy artillery bombardment on the Enemy in front of 1st 36th Divn in front. Gas was discharged on the Somme front at 5 P.M. today.	
	1 Dec 1916.		Indirect fire was carried out last night. Pett. B.015 was we hope suffering. 6500 rounds were fired in all. The day has passed quite quietly. Weather is frosty and a dust must have been hanging all day. The enemy commander was expected round the billets & stables today but we are disappointed however tomorrow a list from the Divisional Commander will no doubt compensate us for our work.	

WAR DIARY FOR MONTH OF DECEMBER, 1916.

VOLUME

48th Machine Gun Coy.

Army Form C. 2118.

WAR DIARY
or
INTELLIGENCE SUMMARY
(Erase heading not required.)

Place	Date	Hour	Summary of Events and Information	Remarks and references to Appendices
VIERSTRAAT Section	1/12/16		In which fire was carried out last night. PETIT BOIS was helped suffering 65 O.R. rounds were fired in all. The day has passed quite quietly. Weather is frosty and a damp mist has been hanging all day. The Army Commander has expected round the Brick Stables to-day but we are disappointed. Known to morrow crowd from the Divisional Commander but no doubt complimented us for our work.	
	2/12/16		Very frosty & clear. The General (49th Div.) called in the morning & went round the B.O.C. This was not [?] after all. O.C. went to Bn. officer to received details of taking over from 49th Bn. M.G. Coy with its Lewis Gun section etc. 49th M.G. Coy takeover with my deputies the very rich attacking to give up his recently constructed dug out in Kemmel. Arrangements for moving with him to morrow at 10.a.m. Coy played a football match with 1st Corp. Cyclists and lost 6 to 1. 9:45pm Gas alarm signals north east rifle distance. No officers' alarm received here	

Army Form C. 2118.

WAR DIARY
or
INTELLIGENCE SUMMARY.
(Erase heading not required.)

Place	Date	Hour	Summary of Events and Information	Remarks and references to Appendices
KLONDYKE Fm.	3/12/16		Weather still frosty. 90th O.C. 49 Coy rang up that nights operations previously cancelled. O.C. 49 is now taking over our 6 rifle guns and an A.A. gun. Our own and 47 Coy guns on the left. Divided O.C. 47 and made all arrangements. Relief of 49 Coy to commence at 9.30 am.	
	4/12/16		Leaders party this morning – a little rain this afternoon. 49 M.G. Coy relieved 3 guns on the right, the relief FORT CALGARY. The other two guns on the right cannot and will. 2nd Section relieved 6 guns of 47 Coy and remaining 3 guns from our own. Relief complete 4.12 noon. Gunnt disposition:– 1 Gun FORT CALGARY. 1 Gun O.P. ROSIGNOL WOOD. 1 Gun GOETHALS Farm and S? gun & area lake over from 47 Coy on the left. Two and H.Q. at BASSE '36 Fm. And 3 Sections at KLONDYKE Fm.	
		6.30 pm	A M[r] Jolly from the KIMMEL Y.M.C.A. had brought down his Cinematograph machine to KLONDYKE Farm and a gave a show of about 7 films in the large barn. This was quite a great diversion especially for the men just out of the trenches. The films therefore were mostly of comic non a short tout of the war promised to come again.	

T2134. (Wt. W708–776. 500,000. 4/15. Sir J. C. & S.

WAR DIARY
or
INTELLIGENCE SUMMARY

Army Form C. 2118.

Place	Date	Hour	Summary of Events and Information	Remarks and references to Appendices
KLONDYKE FARM	5/12/16		Muggy wet day. All guns in their new positions have settled down and have been worried. Indirect fire was carried out last night on enemy communication. 3000 rounds were fired. Our own artillery have been very active to-day.	
	6/12/16		Weather fine but damp. Corps commander visited our transport lines and appears to be quite pleased. Indirect fire was carried out last night on enemy communication. 7500 rounds fired from four guns.	
	7/12/16		Very foggy. New action reconnoitred by C.O. and 2nd/Adair with a view to reorganising the guns in the line. Lieut. Laws the mint joined us. Indirect fire by 15" guns last night harmed 9250 rounds as the Bosh.	
	8/12/16		Still very foggy. Not clear enough to handle to observe enfilade emplacements. Lt Knight & Lt D Edwards reconnoitered their new action with C.O. The General visited us this afternoon. Lots of improvements must be made.	

WAR DIARY
or
INTELLIGENCE SUMMARY

Army Form C. 2118.

Place	Date	Hour	Summary of Events and Information	Remarks and references to Appendices
MONDYKE FARM	8/7/16	5.15pm	Enemy suddenly opened barrage fire of Whizbangs, Trench Mortars and Machine Gun in vicinity of VAN KEEP and TURNERSTOWN LEFT lasting for about 5 mins. Our M.G's retaliated vigorously, expecting a raid.	
	9/7/16		2nd FANSHAWE returned from leave to U.K. Guns.- the Huns kept up fire all night firing 7500 rounds. Quiet day. Improvements being carried out in Billets. Have decided to keep other equipment for the guard and have polished up from position etc.	
	10/7/16		Orders for inspection out last night. 5000 rounds were fired. Wet muddy day. 2/day the Huns shelled KEMMEL with a few H.E. & HE Shrapnel.	
	11/7/16		Major Mayes took over the Brigade. Hot afternoon. Direct fire was carried out during the night, 3250 rounds were fired. Water Section relief was carried out during the morning. O.C. Coy attends opening concert YMCA hut.	

WAR DIARY
or
INTELLIGENCE SUMMARY
(Erase heading not required.)

Army Form C. 2118.

Place	Date	Hour	Summary of Events and Information	Remarks and references to Appendices
KLONDYKE FARM	8/2/16		Shrouded rained all day. Rayhaven quickly last night. 3250 rounds expended at Enemy Communications. The rayhaven replies to them, but when he does fires shots appear to be at random.	
	9/2/16		Quiet by day but very misty. All very quiet in the line. Enemy fire was carried on last night. 5000 rounds were fired. 150ft and then proceeded on leave to day.	
	10/2/16	10 a	Lt. Col Wylie the Corps M.G.O. visited us in the morning and was apparently quite pleased with everything.	
		10 p	Lt. Mulholme returned from leave to U.K. Last night in the line was quiet. Enemies fire was carried out 4250 rounds were fired	

WAR DIARY
or
INTELLIGENCE SUMMARY.
(Erase heading not required.)

Army Form C. 2118.

Instructions regarding War Diaries and Intelligence Summaries are contained in F. S. Regs., Part II. and the Staff Manual respectively. Title pages will be prepared in manuscript.

Place	Date	Hour	Summary of Events and Information	Remarks and references to Appendices
VIERSTRAAT SECTION	15/12/16		There was some enemy artillery activity to-day. It has been very dull and wet all day. The billets are being improved very gradually. There is a great lack of material for hutting and necessary comforts.	
	16/12/16		The enemy were very active this morning in the vicinity of K.1.A. with rifle grenades and trench mortars doing a certain amount of damage to our trenches. Their operations soon caused casualties. Three wounded men were joined in directly lasting AV. The day has been bright and quite warm.	
	17/12/16		The day has passed quietly. Three hundred and fifty rounds were fired last night at GRAND BOIS and UNNAMED WOOD. The relief took place to-day and was completed by 12 noon.	
	18/12/16		The enemy shelled VANDAMME F.H. at intervals during the day. We carried out desultory fire last night firing 3500 rounds. Capt. C.L. ROBERTS went to leave to-day but had to return owing to congested traffic at BOULOGNE.	

Army Form C. 2118.

WAR DIARY
or
INTELLIGENCE SUMMARY.
(Erase heading not required.)

Instructions regarding War Diaries and Intelligence Summaries are contained in F.S. Regs., Part II. and the Staff Manual respectively. Title pages will be prepared in manuscript.

Place	Date	Hour	Summary of Events and Information	Remarks and references to Appendices
VIERSTRAAT SECTION	19/12/16		The day has passed quietly. Last night we fired 3250 rounds into PETIT BOIS, UNNAMED WOOD and by 7 SCHMRTZ WOOD. Today the G.S.O. II and the B.M. Major L.I. Inf. Bde made a tour of the M.G. positions and appeared fairly satisfied. Snow started to fall at about 3.45 P.M. today but it only lasted half an hour.	
	20/12/16		The day has been very cold and clear. Our artillery carried out a continued "strafe" with their field heavy guns. We fired 3750 rounds into the woods. Maintained in yesterday's entry. Capt. ROBERTS went on leave today for ten days.	
	21/12/16		The day has passed quietly. We carried out harassing fire last night firing 3250 rounds. It has snowed practically all day.	
	22/12/16		The day has passed quietly. It has snowed all the morning and hindered work on the positions badly. We fired 4500 rounds into UNNAMED WOOD at 2.30 P.M. in Cavalry were observed a	
	23/12/16		The guns at R.1 dispersed working party in UNNAMED WOOD at 2.30 P.M. in Cavalry were observed a We fired 4250 rounds lasting the	

WAR DIARY or INTELLIGENCE SUMMARY

Army Form C. 2118.

Place	Date	Hour	Summary of Events and Information	Remarks and references to Appendices
VIERSTRAAT SECTION.	24/12/16		Hostile aircraft were unusually active this morning. We carried out I.E. last night firing 4000 rounds. The day has been very snowy and warm.	
	25/12/16		The day started with very frosty weather but about 2 P.M. the wind lowered and the sun came out. The men were hung a dinner tonight to celebrate Christmas. In due course carried out last night.	
	26/12/16		The day has passed quietly. The weather has taken a turn for the worse tonight, rain is falling. Head Quarters & Transport had their Xmas dinner tonight. No intercourse was carried out last night as per Brigade instructions.	
	27/12/16		There was an organised Trench Mortar "shoot" this afternoon. We carried out Indirect fire last night 6500 rounds were fired. The enemy fired about ten rounds of H.V. shells into the vicinity of the Sig. Bn. HQ tents in KEMMEL.	
	28/12/16		The G.O.C. Brigade inspected all the Gun positions today and seemed fairly satisfied. There was a large fire in one of the hutments of the 49th Inf. Bde. about 5:30 P.M. today. We fired 5500 rounds last night.	
	29/12/16		The Corps M.G. Officer Lt. Col. Bythe & O.C. 108 Bn inspected all the Gun positions of this and the 49 R. Inf. Bde. The day has been very mild. We fired 4500 rounds last night indirectly.	
	30/12/16		The day has passed quietly. Indirect fire was carried out last night. 3560 rounds were fired. The weather has been very bad all day.	

Army Form C. 2118.

WAR DIARY
or
INTELLIGENCE SUMMARY
(Erase heading not required.)

Place	Date	Hour	Summary of Events and Information	Remarks and references to Appendices
MERSTRAAT SECTION	31/12/16		The morning passed quietly. This afternoon the enemy shelled with vicinity of PARROT TRENCH with slight and heavy shells. Listening patrols could not notice fire, paying particular attention to some new enemy trenches in the vicinity of Black Cot. D/B'echoes had been Christmas dinner this evening and appeared to enjoy themselves.	

WAR DIARY for month of JANUARY, 1917.

VOLUME 10

148th Machine Gun Coy

WAR DIARY
or
INTELLIGENCE SUMMARY

Army Form C. 2118.

ORIGINAL WAR DIARY

OF

48 M.G. COY

FOR

JANUARY 1917

C.R.Black Capt.
O.C. 48. M.Gun Coy

Vol. IX

SECRET

WAR DIARY or INTELLIGENCE SUMMARY

Army Form C. 2118.

Place	Date	Hour	Summary of Events and Information	Remarks and references to Appendices
VIERSTRAAT SECTION	1/1/1917		The day has passed quietly. During the day was carried out last night, 3250 rounds were fired on the BOIS DE WYTSCHAETE and PETIT BOIS and UNNAMED WOOD.	
	2/1/17		A combined T.M. J M.G. and Artillery bombardment took place today on the attached table. The German front line suffered badly. The machine guns fired 6375 rounds in the 90 minutes rate. The enemy retaliated with 5.9s, 4.2s and 1.7 shrapnel. No casualties were sustained by his activity. Some shell burst very near the M.G. position and against S.P.13. We had a level knocking but no doubt the Germans will learn to respect our T.M.s after today's "Strafe". Captain Roberts returned from leave yesterday. In addition we carried out last night 3250 rounds were fired.	
	3/1/17		Colonel Wyatt visited the Company this morning and appeared very pleased with everything. Lt. Christie honours Rewards appeared in Gazette today, Sgt FEVER has been awarded the Distinguished Conduct Medal. He carried out ordinary fire last night firing 2000 rounds.	
	4/1/17		The day has passed quietly. It commenced with rain but cleared off about midday and the sun shone well for the rest of the day. Last night a small reconnaissance party entered the German front line and gathered a certain amount of information. The Pioneer of No. 6 Company took to "A" and "B" last night ready to fire upon Lodrage Roads the attack by the enemy be attempted as they were expected.	

Army Form C. 2118.

WAR DIARY
or
INTELLIGENCE SUMMARY.
(Erase heading not required.)

Instructions regarding War Diaries and Intelligence Summaries are contained in F. S. Regs., Part II. and the Staff Manual respectively. Title pages will be prepared in manuscript.

Place	Date	Hour	Summary of Events and Information	Remarks and references to Appendices
VIEARSTRAAT SECTION.	5/1/17		The day and night passed quietly. We carried out indirect fire last night firing 600 rounds on PETIT BOIS, GRAND BOIS and the SONNEN ROAD. Enemy aircraft more active today.	
"	6/1/17		The day has passed quietly. We carried out indirect fire last night firing 2000 rounds.	
	7/1/17		One of our airplanes came to grief this morning. It was seen to descend well under control but in flames. It had 7500 rounds in magazine. Our artillery was active last night and the enemy shelled VIERSTRAAT this morning.	
	8/1/17		We carried out indirect fire last night firing 3000 rounds. Lt Col. WYLIE looked at the CINCHA LOCRE Machine Guns this morning. The G.O.C. Division appeared much pleased.	
	9/1/17		The day has been very dull but dangerous. The enemy was very active with his artillery and the has been doing some damage. We fired 3000 rounds indirectly last night. There was a tat. S.O.S. this afternoon at 2.30 P.M. everything satisfactory.	
	10/1/17		An enemy aeroplane flew over Kemy at about 3.40 P.M. today and fired at our Observation Balloon with its Machine Gun. This caused the Observation Officers to descend hurriedly in their parachutes and the Balloon to descend in flames. The little plane got back to its own lines safely. Today a 4:2 shell alighted & burst on the dugout at No 3. M.G. but did no damage.	

T2134. Wt. W708-776. 50000. 4/15. Sir J. C. & S.

WAR DIARY or INTELLIGENCE SUMMARY

Army Form C. 2118.

Place	Date	Hour	Summary of Events and Information	Remarks and references to Appendices
VIERSTRAAT Section PETIT BOIS	11/1/17		The day & night passed quietly. The enemy section retaliated Plans & M.G. bullets by T.M. The weather has been very cold & sleet falling most of the day. We fired 2000 rounds on enemy during the night.	
	12/1/17		The day & night passed quietly with the exception of a certain amount of enemy activity during the night. The enemy cut enfiladed M.G. through the night & fired 2500 rounds. Enemy M.G's retaliated on M.G's that had been firing.	
	13/1/17		A very quiet day & night. Test shooting carried out in the trenches and registered on Enemy jumping off place in the trenches. Received a visit from the Brigadier this afternoon. Indirect fire carried out during the night, 3750 rounds being fired.	
	14/1/17		The day then passed quietly. The weather has been frosty and the roads are very slippery. Today the men were busy cleaning of the camp for the inspection tomorrow by the G.O.C. 2nd ARMY.	
	15/1/17		The weather broke very cold all & this. The G.O.C. 2nd ARMY did not visit this company owing to everybody's aircraft inactivity. Everything had been prepared & a great amount of extra work to be carried out throughout the last night.	
	16/1/17		The day has passed quietly on our front though there has been considerable artillery activity on our left. The day has been cold & nothing there to report though the have been considerable artillery activity on our left. The day has been cold & nothing to report. All the available officers & N.C.O's attended a lecture this morning by the C.pt. Machine Gun Officer.	

Army Form C. 2118.

WAR DIARY
or
INTELLIGENCE SUMMARY.
(Erase heading not required.)

Instructions regarding War Diaries and Intelligence Summaries are contained in F. S. Regs., Part II. and the Staff Manual respectively. Title pages will be prepared in manuscript.

Place	Date	Hour	Summary of Events and Information	Remarks and references to Appendices
VIERSTRAAT SECTION	17/1/17		There is no enemy activity to record today. The snow has been falling fast all day. The men who were relieved today. A snow hall typhoon arrived between E & D sections this afternoon. The only casualties being a few numerous cap badges.	
	18/1/17		The day has passed quietly. More snow fell today. This afternoon the two sections in rest went into WEST OUTRE for baths.	
	19/1/17		The enemy have been active with artillery during the day. I don't fire were carried out last night. 3000 rounds were fired on points behind the HOSPICE.	
	20/1/17		The weather is frightfully cold today to see. We organised a football match this afternoon for the Company. The enemy has not been active today. He carried out no work last night.	
	21/1/17		The day has been very cold. The enemy were fairly active with their artillery. They had the 49 F.A.BRIGADE ORCH. The Officers Quarters at BASSETTE FARM were in another. Collapsing and a move will have to be made elsewhere. We carried on ahead. Our last night firing 6000 rounds.	
	22/1/17		Today has been very cold. There has been a great amount of Artillery activity on the right front of the ULSTER Div. hrs whether it is hostile or otherwise it is impossible to say. We carried out indirect fire last night on enemy's communications.	

T2134. Wt. W708—776. 500000. 4/15. Sir J. C. & S.

WAR DIARY
or
INTELLIGENCE SUMMARY.
(Erase heading not required.)

Army Form C. 2118.

Place	Date	Hour	Summary of Events and Information	Remarks and references to Appendices
VIERSTRAAT 23 SECTION	1/1/17		There is nothing to report. A new officer reinforced the Company today 2/Lt. TAYLOR. The patrols were in force. We carried out two recces last night on UNNAMED WOOD. Yesterday we dispersed a German carrying party in UNNAMED WOOD.	
	2/1/17		Two enemy aeroplanes passed over our lines today 15m were used to fight to warrant any M.G. A.A. firing from us. The enemy shelled the vicinity of PARRET TRENCH this afternoon firing some fixed shooting landing a 4.2 mm. immediately behind No.5 M.G. dugout. A football match between the Officers & N.C.Os. v. the MEN took place this afternoon in which the MEN won by 2 to 1 goals.	
	25/1/17		The weather has remained very cold and we come to the morning. The enemy have been active with T.M.s and M.Gs last night.	
	26/1/17		Weather still frosty. Great aerial activity today. Indirect persons carried out last up AT 56.00 rounds were fired.	
	27/1/17		Hostile T.M.s were active on the CENTRE BRIGADE FRONT LINE this afternoon. We carried out Indirect Fire last night firing 5150 rounds on our targets. Weather still freezing.	

Army Form C. 2118.

WAR DIARY
or
INTELLIGENCE SUMMARY.
(Erase heading not required.)

Instructions regarding War Diaries and Intelligence Summaries are contained in F. S. Regs., Part II. and the Staff Manual respectively. Title pages will be prepared in manuscript.

Place	Date	Hour	Summary of Events and Information	Remarks and references to Appendices
VIERSTRAAT SECTION	28/1/17		Last night four guns in the line did accurate shoots on the VIERSTRAAT - WYTSCHAETE Road & Trench Rly. from GRAND BOIS to WYTSCHAETE. opening fire simultaneously at 6.30 p.m., 7.30 p.m. & 8.0 p.m. then continuing at varying intervals throughout the night. Enemy Artillery has been active to-day. Cold weather still continuing.	
	29/1/17		The weather is still freezing. An enemy Aeroplane flew over our lines to-day but was soon driven back. The said that 20 degrees below zero is the present temperature.	
	30/1/17		The temperature today is about the lowest we have had since this weather set in. It has snowed intermittently through to-day. The greatest snow was about 6 inches.	
	31/1/17		Shrapnel in the direction of BUTTERFLY FARM but about 3¾ ya hide short. The snow started today. The Company CANTEEN will start tomorrow having stocked this evening. There is nothing to report.	

WAR DIARY.

FOR MONTH OF FEBRUARY, 1917.

VOLUME 11

UNIT:- 48th Machine Gun Company.

C H Roberts
Capt
OC 48th Gun Coy.

Army Form C. 2118.

WAR DIARY
or
INTELLIGENCE SUMMARY.
(Erase heading not required.)

Place	Date	Hour	Summary of Events and Information	Remarks and references to Appendices
WYTSCHAETE SECTOR.	1/7/17		Men willing if an portive to rile. The enemy attempted to raid the A.7.13 & A.16 & E Posts but without success being driven back by the Lewis Gunners. The Cheshires opened today for the first time with success.	
	2/7/17		We carried out a barrage in answer to enemy heavy barrage from Klondyke F.R. All the guns were actually ready to open fire on the position allotted them within two hours and 5 minutes.	
	3/7/17		The day has been fairly quiet. Some aerial activity. The weather is very dull today.	
	4/7/17		The day from General point of view. Last night we were the attackers & got in one end of the number. The relief took place today.	
	5/7/17		The day has passed finally on our front. The aeroplanes were very active this afternoon. Spotting for our heavy artillery. Our artillery fire was carried out about 3,400 rounds fired.	
	6/7/17		The enemy sent over two Shells up to 5.9 Calibre at two of our guns just 200 yards away from this Farm. The railway was hit in about 6 places but the guns were not scratched although some of the shells burst right under neath the muzzles of the guns. Pieces fell about on the Farm but no damage was done. The Fire appears to have started no Retaliation expected and once again. The work here was carried out last night	

Army Form C. 2118.

WAR DIARY
or
INTELLIGENCE SUMMARY.
(Erase heading not required.)

Instructions regarding War Diaries and Intelligence Summaries are contained in F.S. Regs., Part II. and the Staff Manual respectively. Title pages will be prepared in manuscript.

Place	Date	Hour	Summary of Events and Information	Remarks and references to Appendices
VIERSTRAAT SECTION.	7/2/17		There is nothing of importance to note to-day. The old weather continues.	
	8/2/17.		The enemy sent over a considerable number of shells into Kemmel Shelters Camp. Comparatively few casualties. During the day we found, firstly, we sent out Indirect fire last night on PETR 8013 and the VIERSTRAAT — WYTSCHAETE ROAD. firing 3500 rounds.	
	9/2/17.		The day has been quiet. Indirect fire was carried out at night. The Company practised reinforcing the line last night with the eight guns & learn in no event the Alarm was received in the Officers Mess at Tea line. Allowed him within this exactly 2 hours & 10 minute from the time the Alarm was received in the Officers Mess at Tea line.	
	10/2/17.		The artillery seem to have had a shoot this morning at 10.30. AM. This shoot and take place. The enemy shelled a 4.5 How. Bty heavily this morning, doing no material damage. One of our I.E. patrols was rather allured in shape after receiving a visit lit but this will be easily repaired. A new Officer is reported to this Company to-day, 2/Lt OSWIN. Indirect fire was carried out last night. 3000 rounds being fired in two Dumps at O.13.c.70.70. and O.19.c.50.65.	

T.2134. Wt. W708-776. 500,000. 4/15. Sir J. C. & S.

WAR DIARY
or
INTELLIGENCE SUMMARY.
(Erase heading not required.)

Army Form C. 2118.

Place	Date	Hour	Summary of Events and Information	Remarks and references to Appendices
VIERSTRAAT Section	14/3/17		A clear bright day but little enemy aeroplane activity. Gradual thaw continues. Gratitude to Sergeant Bamrick left the Company & No 35 Coy & No 35 Coy as Sergt-Maj. Rather a large percentage of men reporting sick but no cases of trench feet. About 4000 rounds were fired during the night on roads behind enemy lines.	
"	15/3/17		The day passed quietly. About 8pm, four guns with men to work them were warned to be in readiness to move off. At twenty minutes past eight they were ready & 20 any orders and to do anything. Guns were placed along road from B.H.Q. to here in positions suitable for anti aircraft shooting. Guns remained mounted till 7am the following morning. No aeroplanes were seen.	
"	16/3/17		Pond changed and much warmer. Large numbers of our planes up. About 5000 rounds were fired during the night on Road in rear of HOSPICE and PETIT BOIS.	

Army Form C. 2118.

WAR DIARY
or
INTELLIGENCE SUMMARY.
(Erase heading not required.)

Instructions regarding War Diaries and Intelligence Summaries are contained in F.S. Regs., Part II. and the Staff Manual respectively. Title pages will be prepared in manuscript.

Place	Date	Hour	Summary of Events and Information	Remarks and references to Appendices
VIERSTRAAT SECTION.	11/2/17.		YORK ROAD was heavily gas-shelled last night. Again at about 12 NOON today the enemy gas-shelled the same neighbourhood. The X. Corps bombarded GRAND BOIS. To-day. Lieut. MULHOLLAND has been appointed to No. 109 MACHINE GUN COMPANY and bids farewell to the 49th M. GUN COMPANY. Lieut BANNISTER has been appointed 2nd in COMMAND and no doubt he will fulfil his arduous duties excellently. He carried out work on the VIERSTRAAT - WYTSCHAETE ROADS, about 3000 rounds were expended.	
"	12/2/17		The day & night passed quietly. We carried out indirect fire traversing the road to Coft Ipoire. About 4000 rounds were fired. Lieut Mulholland did not leave as expected.	
"	13/2/17.		Lieut MULHOLLAND proceeded today 6.7.16 on take command of No. 109 MACHINE GUN COMPANY.	

WAR DIARY
or
INTELLIGENCE SUMMARY

Army Form C. 2118.

Place	Date	Hour	Summary of Events and Information	Remarks and references to Appendices
VIERSTRAAT SECTION	17/3/17		A misty day. A and B sections came down from line being relieved by C & D sections. A & B came in for a certain amount of shelling in York Road near Ara woods. About 500 rounds were fired on Sunken Road, Dump near Hospice and Petit Bois. Our heavies did a lot of shooting today. Section Officers have moved to another billet pending the arrival of the child & children which the momentarily expected at their billet.	
"	18/3/17		Another misty day. Our heavies did a shoot during the afternoon — two direct hits were reported on the SOUTHERN BRICKSTACK. 350 rounds were fired during the night.	
"	19/3/17		R.E. started putting new roof on barn where men are billeted. Some of the kitchens and mules in many of the units we expect take off their food. Men are all right at present.	

Army Form C. 2118.

WAR DIARY
or
INTELLIGENCE SUMMARY.
(Erase heading not required.)

Place	Date	Hour	Summary of Events and Information	Remarks and references to Appendices
VIERSTRAAT SECTION.	22/3/17		Rained all day. Our heavies & T.Ms active all the time. 1500 rounds M.G fire on WYTSCHAETE WOOD. Enemy retaliates for artillery strafe on trenches behind YORK ROAD.	
"	23/3/17		A thick mist day. Thaw restrictions still in force. Work in the trenches delayed by condition of ground. As much drainage is possible is being carried out. Indirect fire 3500 rounds on trenches and unnamed wood which had been bombarded during the day by our heavies.	
"	24/3/17		Indirect fire was carried out during the night. No rain but thick mist.	
"	25/3/17		Good progress is being made in work on the trenches. Our heavies continue a deliberate bombardment of enemy trenches. Indirect fire carried out on RAILWAY JUNCTIONS near HOSPICE and PETIT BOIS.	

Army Form C. 2118.

WAR DIARY
or
INTELLIGENCE SUMMARY.
(Erase heading not required.)

Place	Date	Hour	Summary of Events and Information	Remarks and references to Appendices
VIERSTRAAT Section.	24/5/17		A & B Sections relieved C & D sections. We formed guards on ammunition dumps. We cooperated with 124 Bty in gunis indirect fire for raid on our left firing 14500 rounds on GRAND BOIS, NAIL ROW TRENCH (N18 B) and HOLLANDSCHESCHOUR SALIENT.	
"	25/5/17		Quiet on our front. Muggy weather and warmer.	
"	26/5/17		Clear weather. Some enemy artillery activity on our front. Destructive on cannot not 6 our guns. 3000 rounds being fired on HAMED DRIVE up to M. HOSPICE and 1000 rounds afterwards from HOSPICE to left corner of UNNAMED WOOD.	

Army Form C. 2118.

WAR DIARY
or
INTELLIGENCE SUMMARY.
(Erase heading not required.)

Place	Date	Hour	Summary of Events and Information	Remarks and references to Appendices
VIERSTRAAT SECTION	27/2/17		Indirect fire was carried out during the night. 3000 rounds being fired enfilading NAME DRIVE. 1000 rounds traversing from HOSPICE to left of UNNAMED WOOD. Enemy quiet during day & night. Roads beginning to lift, owing to thaw.	
"	28/2/17		Indirect fire was carried out during the night. 4500 rounds being fired. The batteries went round positions with C.O. and all ranks of staff including a Cheshire General were met with. The R.E's are making good progress on the billets. The old cook house has been condemned by R.E's and a new one is being built by them. The dairy here was painted today by HETHERSAY.	

Childwick
Capt.
O.i/c 48th Gun Coy.

WAR DIARY
FOR MONTH OF MARCH, 1917.

VOLUME 12

UNIT:- 48th Machine Gun Company.

Vol. XI

WAR DIARY or INTELLIGENCE SUMMARY

Army Form C. 2118.

Place	Date	Hour	Summary of Events and Information	Remarks and references to Appendices
VIERSTRAAT Sector	1/3/17		Indirect fire was carried out during the night. 3500 rounds on NAMED DRIVE, 2500 on PETIT BOIS, 1000 traversing from HOSPICE to left of UNNAMED WOOD. Aerial activity went unobserved.	
	2/3/17		The 87th Company carried out workers rations at the Range 12 rounds for each man. C & D sections relieved A & B. Indirect fire was carried out during the night. 2500 rounds traversing from HOSPICE & NORTHERN BRICKSTACK. 1000 rounds traversing from HOSPICE to left of UNNAMED WOOD. No change in the Stables yet.	
	3/3/17		A Misty day after a cold & frosty night. The Brigadier inspected lines & Mules and billets. R.E.s are making good progress with work on billets. A wire was thrown to the Brigade front on our right. Indirect fire was carried out during the night. [illegible] caring through our trenches.	

Army Form C. 2118.

WAR DIARY
or
INTELLIGENCE SUMMARY.
(Erase heading not required.)

Place	Date	Hour	Summary of Events and Information	Remarks and references to Appendices
VIERSTRAAT Sector.	4/3/17		A bright clear day. Considerable aerial activity on our part. A new officer Lt. Gatesby joined the Company from the base. 1 O.R. made our strength from D.A.C. Indirect fire was carried out during the night.	
"	5/3/17		Fairly heavy snow during the day followed by thaw. The wet critch officers that have the gun up were inspected by the hygiene. Indirect fire was carried out during the night. Fresh H.Q. moved into new dug out at the Farm. New dug out at the MOUND was also occupied today.	
"	6/3/17		Drew a fresh L.D. man from 47th Mobile Veterinary. Indirect fire was carried out during the night in futhner. 2000 rounds on ONTREAT WOOD 1000 rounds on PETIT BOIS	

WAR DIARY or INTELLIGENCE SUMMARY

Army Form C. 2118.

Place	Date	Hour	Summary of Events and Information	Remarks and references to Appendices
VIERSTRAAT SECTOR	7/5/17		Artillery cold wind. Co. went round the line before breakfast. A train at the back of every line on the trolley track. Lt. Gatley returned to the Coy from Hospital. Inclusion of prisoners carried out during the night 2000 rounds on Communication Trenches and 2000 on NORTH HOUSES.	
	8/5/17		Indirect fire was carried out during the night on WYTSCHAETE WOOD and NORTH HOUSE. At 5.30 pm enemy artillery opened up important support line; all M.Gs started to rapid fire on No 3 Barrage. Some live shells fell behind YPRES ROAD, but shell did not affect our position.	
	9/5/17		Every wind is said to come first on the night 8/5/9/5. The following is the report received from 2nd Lt Shields and 2nd Lt TAYLOR in charge of M.Gs on the line:— During the enemy preliminary bombardment the guns all started to but shot notified on any barrage line, but the instant the S.O.S signal at about 9pm at 2nd Lt BYARDS decided to open fire on No 3 Barrage. He found	

WAR DIARY or INTELLIGENCE SUMMARY

Army Form C. 2118.

Place	Date	Hour	Summary of Events and Information	Remarks and references to Appendices
VIERSTRAAT SECTOR	8/3/17	Continued	The signal for this from our guns had within 30 seconds at least 5 guns had opened fire. The enemy engaged MG4 and MG7 with MG fire but did no damage. It was impossible to turn our fire. All guns were asked to keep up a continuous fire on No 3 Barrage but to keep a good watch for sign of an attack from any direction. At M.G.5 Corporal ALLEN turned his enemy M.G. firing from a point between the S corner of UNNAMED WOOD and SOUTHERN BACKSTACK. He engaged this gun and shortly afterwards a shell was seen to burst at this point after which the enemy gun was silent. At 8.10 p.m. the signal to stand to down was fired from No 9 M.G. and firing stopped. At 4.10 a.m. this morning the enemy opened up a barrage. All guns stood to & opened at once. S.O.S. signal was observed on our right front and fire was again opened on No 3 Barrage. 2 guns also fired behind MAEDELSTEED FARM as the enemy was reported to be massing there. Fire was stopped at 6.40 a.m. The number of rounds fired in each occasion was — 8 p.m. to 8.10 p.m. 11,500 rounds. 4.10 a.m. to 6.40 a.m. 3,750 "	

Army Form C. 2118.

WAR DIARY
or
INTELLIGENCE SUMMARY.
(Erase heading not required.)

Instructions regarding War Diaries and Intelligence Summaries are contained in F. S. Regs., Part II. and the Staff Manual respectively. Title pages will be prepared in manuscript.

Place	Date	Hour	Summary of Events and Information	Remarks and references to Appendices
VIERSTRAAT SECTOR	10/3/17		Indirect fire was carried out during the night. 3000 rounds on NANCY DRIVE 200 rounds on UNNAMED WOOD 3000 rounds on NAP RESERVE TRENCH at 5.10 pm all teams stood to and M.G.2 opened fire on region behind HAEDELSTEEDE FARM. At 5.30 pm. Enemy trench down.	
	11/3/17		Enemy was reported this morning behind MAEDELSTEEDE FARM all guns stood to at 5.10 am. 5250 rounds were fired into this area. Stand down at 5.55 pm. Indirect fire was carried out during the night to district in enemy relief that was reported the battalion to occupy to last 5.45 am 18750 rounds were fired on communications in PETIT BOIS, UNNAMED WOOD and GRAND BOIS, YORK ROAD was shelled during the afternoon.	
	12/3/17		Indirect fire was carried out during the night on NAME DRIVE and between MAEPDELSTEEDE FARM. 4000 rounds in all. Enemy was quiet during the night.	

Army Form C. 2118.

WAR DIARY
or
INTELLIGENCE SUMMARY.
(Erase heading not required.)

Instructions regarding War Diaries and Intelligence Summaries are contained in F. S. Regs., Part II. and the Staff Manual respectively. Title pages will be prepared in manuscript.

Place	Date	Hour	Summary of Events and Information	Remarks and references to Appendices
VIERSTRAAT Sector.	13/5/17		Indirect fire was carried out during the night. 7500 rounds being fired on GRAND BOIS, NORTHERN to SOUTHERN BRICKSTACK and PETIT BOIS. 109th M.G.Coy took over from 49th M.G.Coy on our right. Three Vickers guns were handed in by us today.	
	14/5/17		C.D Sections relieved A and B Sections in the trenches. Indirect fire was carried out during the night. 5500 rounds were fired on PETIT BOIS, and between NORTHERN and SOUTHERN Buckstack and on GRAND BOIS.	
	15/5/17		Indirect fire was carried out during the night. 1000 rounds on WYTSCHAETE WOOD 3500 rounds on railway from HOSPICE to South END of GRAND BOIS also on WYTSCHAETE WOOD.	

Army Form C. 2118.

WAR DIARY
or
INTELLIGENCE SUMMARY.
(Erase heading not required.)

Instructions regarding War Diaries and Intelligence Summaries are contained in F. S. Regs, Part II. and the Staff Manual respectively. Title pages will be prepared in manuscript.

Place	Date	Hour	Summary of Events and Information	Remarks and references to Appendices
WIERSTRAAT Sector	16/5/17		Intermittent fire was carried out during the night on WYTSCHAETE WOOD. 3000 rounds were fired.	
	17/5/17		Indirect fire was carried out last night WYTSCHAETE WOOD, PETIT BOIS and UNNAMED WOOD. 6000 rounds were fired. Enemy fired about 12 shrapnel over FORT HALIFAX, also registering on PARRAT TRENCH and one between this and BRVKGRIE.	
	18/5/17		Indirect fire was carried out during the night on WYTSCHAETE WOOD and UNNAMED WOOD. 3000 rounds were fired. At about 2.30 p.m. section in the hire crept two teams at HALIFAX and M.G.7 were relieved by 49th M.G. Coy. Owing to visibility being good teams at HALIFAX and BRVKERIE (M.G.7) were not relieved till dusk. At 2.30 p.m. Coy H.Q. Posts A and B sections and transport moved from KLONDIKE FARM to SCHERPENBERG. 49th M.G. Coy took over these lines and transport billets at KLONDIKE. The hive over carried out satisfactorily.	See Appendix 1

T.2134. Wt. W708-776. 500000. 4/15. Sir J. C. & S.

Army Form C. 2118.

WAR DIARY
or
INTELLIGENCE SUMMARY.
(Erase heading not required.)

Place	Date	Hour	Summary of Events and Information	Remarks and references to Appendices
Steenvoorde.	19/3/17		General cleaning up and overhaul of Gun equipment. Transport lines which are bad are being improved. All machine gunners paraded for baths at LOCRE today.	
	20/3/17		G.O.C. inspected the Company this morning at 10.30 also the Transport lines. Gun equipment was noted not and lists of deficiencies made.	
	21/3/17		Clearer weather today. Certain amount of work done in fixing up transport lines. Usual programme of work for the Company carried thro' with usual march from 7 am to 7.45 am.	
	22/3/17		Usual programme of work from 7 am to 5 pm. Football in the afternoon.	

Army Form C. 2118.

WAR DIARY
or
INTELLIGENCE SUMMARY.
(Erase heading not required.)

Instructions regarding War Diaries and Intelligence Summaries are contained in F. S. Regs., Part II. and the Staff Manual respectively. Title pages will be prepared in manuscript.

Place	Date	Hour	Summary of Events and Information	Remarks and references to Appendices
SCHERPENBERG	23/3/17		Following programme of work was carried out:—	
		7 - 7.45 am	6 short march with mask disciplined.	
		9.30 - 10.0 am	A & B sections. Musketeers. 11 am - 12.15 pm Gun drill	
		9.30 - 10.0 am	C & D section. Gun drill. 11 am - 12.15 pm Musketeers.	
		2 - 3 pm	All sections. Topography.	
			Cold weather with some snow.	
	24/3/17	7 am - 7.45	N.C.O. infantry drill. Remainder of Coy short march with mask disciplined.	
		9.30 - 10.0 am	Inspection of Box respirators and gun drill.	
		10.05 - 12.15 pm	Gun drill with box respirators.	
		2 pm - 3 pm	Care & cleaning of guns. Transport Box respirator drill.	
	25/3/17		Warmer weather. Church parade in morning.	
			Football tournament carried on in the afternoon.	
			Summer time started today.	

Army Form C. 2118.

WAR DIARY
or
INTELLIGENCE SUMMARY.
(Erase heading not required.)

Place	Date	Hour	Summary of Events and Information	Remarks and references to Appendices
SCHEAPENBERG	26/3/17	7am – 7.45am	Company march with march discipline. N.C.O's Infantry drill.	
		9am – 10am	Preparation of guns for firing.	
		10am – 12.30pm	Range Firing; no gas masks under gas cloud.	
		2pm – 3pm	Care & cleaning of guns.	
			Football & games remainder of day.	
	27/3/17	7am – 7.45am	March. N.C.O's Infantry drill.	
		A.B. sections: 9am – 10.30am	Section drill.	
		" 10.45 – 12.15pm	Fire direction & control.	
		C. D sections. 9am – 10.30am	Fire direction & Control	
		" 10.45am – 12.15pm	Section drill.	
		2pm – 3pm	Gun drill & fire direction. 3pm Games.	
	28/3/17	7am – 7.45am	March. N.C.O's Infantry Drill	
		9am	Route march.	
		2pm – 3pm	Cleaning personal equipment.	

Army Form C. 2118.

WAR DIARY
or
INTELLIGENCE SUMMARY.
(Erase heading not required.)

Place	Date	Hour	Summary of Events and Information	Remarks and references to Appendices
SCHERPENBERG.	29/3/17	7am - 7.45am	March. N.C.Os Infantry Drill	
			A & B sections. 9am - 10.30am Section drill.	
			10.45am - 12.15pm Fire direction & Control	
			C & D sections. 9am - 10.30am Fire direction & Control	
			10.45am - 12.15pm Section drill	
			2pm - 3pm Packing limbers. 3pm Games.	
"	30/3/17		Company marched off at 9am to proceed to II Army Training Area	Appendix II
HERZEELE.	31/3/17		Operation Orders No 15 & 31-3-17.	
			1. In continuation of O.O. No 15 dated 31-3-17 this company will move to Billets at WIZERNES at the 14th inst as a second stage in the move to Second Army Training Area in accordance with 48th I.B Operation Order No 109. dated 31-3-17.	
			2. Transport will be packed by 8.0 am.	
			3. Billets will be cleaned by J. Seaman	

Army Form C. 2118.

WAR DIARY
or
INTELLIGENCE SUMMARY.
(Erase heading not required.)

Place	Date	Hour	Summary of Events and Information	Remarks and references to Appendices
		cont'd		
	3/3/17		4. Company will parade ready to march off 9.0 a.m. Drew fighting order with water proof sheets folded under the flap of the haversack.	
			The Company reached HAZEBROUCK at 4 p.m. to day.	

R. K. Ravenscroft Lt
for O.C.
48 Machine Gun Coy.

SECRET.   Appendix I.   War Diary
                                    COPY No 3

48 MACHINE GUN COMPANY O.O No 1 4

Ref. SHEET No 28 SW. ED. 4A 1/20,000.   17-3-17.

1. 48 Company Machine Gun Corps will be relieved by 49 Coy. M.G.C. in the VIERSTRAAT Section on the 18 March 1917.

2. **TRENCHES**

(A) One guide per gun will be detailed from Headquarters to meet relieving gun teams at KEMMEL CHATEAU at 1.30 P.M.

(B) Trench stores <u>only</u> will be handed over, and receipts obtained. Forms to be used are issued herewith.

C. MG 7 & 8 will only be relieved in daylight if visibility is bad. Otherwise relief of these two guns will commence at dusk.
Relieving teams will wait at M.G.6 & M.G.3 respectively.
Transport will meet outcoming teams at KEMMEL

D. One man per gun team will be detailed from H.Q. to report at Section H.Q. as a carrying party. Guides will also assist in carrying out.

E. On completion of relief, teams will report at KLONDYKE F.m, and will move in one body to billets at SCHERPENBERG

3. **BILLETS**

(A) 48 M.G. Coy will take over the billets occupied by 49 M.G. Coy at SCHERPENBERG the 18 March 1917.
Blankets will be made up in bundles by gun teams and stacked ready for transport outside Q.M. stores by 7 a.m.

OO14. SHEET II

(C) An advance party will proceed to the new billets with the Q.M. Stores and baggage at 8 am.

(D) Gun equipment will be ready for Transport by 10 AM.

(E) Billets will be thoroughly cleaned, all refuse buried or burned in the incinerator. Latrines will be emptied.

F. All barrack stores will be handed into Q.M Stores by 1.30 P.M.

G. Company will parade, ready to march off at 2 P.M.

COPY N°
1 - OFFICE
2 & 3 - WAR DIARY
4 - "A" SECTION
5 - B "
6 - C "
7 - D "
8 - TRANSPORT.

Ch. Roberts
CAPT
COMD. 48. MG Coy.

Appendix II

SECRET   No. 48 COMPANY. M.G.C.   COPY No. 2

OPERATION ORDER No. 15.   30 MARCH 1917

REF MAP. HAZEBROUCK 5A 1/100,000

1. No. 48 Coy. M.G.C. will move to II ARMY TRAINING AREA, RECQUES in accordance with 48TH INFANTRY BRIGADE OPERATION ORDER No. 108 D/30-3-17.

2. The move will be carried out in three stages. First Stage, on the 31st INST. will be to the vicinity of HAZEBROUCK.

3. The route will be YMCA hut LOCRE – BAILLEUL – CROSS ROADS 400x W. OF BAILLEUL ON BAILLEUL- METEREN RD – STRAZELLE – HAZEBROUCK.

4. A billeting party consisting of LT. J.E. GATELY and No. 27614 SGT. J. PETTICREW will proceed in advance, and report to the staff Captain at the church, LOCRE by 12 NOON 30TH INST.

5(A). Blankets will be packed in bundles by gun teams, labelled and stacked outside the guard-room ready for motor transport by 7AM.

B. The Q.M. Stores will also proceed by motor lorry.

8. The C.Q.M.S. and 2 O.R. will accompany the lorry.

C. All kits will be packed on the limbers by 8 AM.

6. Camp will be cleaned by 8.30 am. All rubbish refuse will be either buried or burned in the incinerator.

7. The company will parade ready to march off at 9. A.M. Order of march as when fighting is imminent, will be as follows:-

A Section followed in succession by B. C. D and transport less A Section's A Echelon.

COPIES TO

No. 1 - FILE
No. 2 & 3. WAR DIARY
No. 4 2nd IN COMD.
No. 5 OC A SECTION
No. 6 " B "
No. 7 " C "
No. 8 " D "
No. 9

CAPT
COMDG. 48 M.G. COY.

WAR DIARY FOR MONTH OF APRIL, 1917.

VOLUME:- 13

UNIT: No 48 Machine Gun Coy

Vol 12

Army Form C. 2118.

WAR DIARY
or
INTELLIGENCE SUMMARY.
(Erase heading not required.)

Instructions regarding War Diaries and Intelligence Summaries are contained in F. S. Regs., Part II. and the Staff Manual respectively. Title pages will be prepared in manuscript.

Place	Date	Hour	Summary of Events and Information	Remarks and references to Appendices
WIZERNES.	1/4/17		The Coy reached WIZERNES at 4.30 p.m. We found good billets for the men.	
	2/4/17		The Coy left WIZERNES at 8.15 a.m. and reached LA PLUOY at 1 p.m. The billets for the men were fairly good but no covered standings for mules. At 6 p.m. all horses & mules were moved to the Mill at RECQUES, where we have excellent standings and billets. Every thing was settled in by 10 p.m.	
	3/4/17		At 2 p.m. the Coy moved from billets at LA PLUOY to fresh billets in RECQUES. The morning was spent in cleaning & overhauling guns and equipment.	
	4/4/17	6.30 – 7.30 a.m. 9 a.m. – 10 a.m. 11 – 12 noon. 12 – 1 p.m.	Cleaning clothing & equipment. C.O's inspection. Stoppages. C.O – N.C.O's direction. Indication & recognition of targets. N.C.O's and N.S.I. Map reading. Remounters on horses.	

T/134. Wt. W708–776. 50000. 4/15. Sir J. C. & S.

Army Form C. 2118.

WAR DIARY
or
INTELLIGENCE SUMMARY.
(Erase heading not required.)

Place	Date	Hour	Summary of Events and Information	Remarks and references to Appendices
RECQUES.	5/4/17	6.30 am – 7.30 am	Cleaning equipment & inspection by section Officers. C.O.'s inspection.	
		9 – 10 am	Stoppages (L.G.) 10 am – 12 noon. T. & G. in Elementary Training.	
		12 – 1 pm	Fire direction. 2 pm. 3½ mile run.	
"	6/4/17	6.30 – 7.30 am	Word inspection. 9 am – 1 pm. A Section Grouping on range.	
			Remainder 9 – 10 am Stoppages. 10 – 11 am Indication & recognition. 11 am – 12 noon Gun drill.	
		12 – 1 pm	Points before, during & after firing. 2 pm. ¼ mile heat for relay race.	
"	7/4/17	6.30 – 7.30 a.m.	As usual. 9 am – 1 pm. B Section Range. Grouping practice. Stoppages.	
			Remainder 9 – 10 a Gun drill. 10 – 11 am Stoppages. 11 am – 12 noon Fire direction.	
		12 noon – 1 pm	Indication & recognition. Fire direction in groups. 2 pm. ½ mile heats contd.	
			Church Parade. 11 am Co's Section Range. Grouping. Stoppages etc.	
"	8/4/17		A & B Section. Use of cover. Choice of ground.	
"	9/4/17	7 am.	Guns reported to Battalions for practice attack.	
"	10/4/17	6.30 – 7.30 am	Stripping & cleaning of equipment. 9.15 am G.O.C.'s inspection.	
"	11/4/17	6.30 – 7.30 am	Usual cleaning of equipment & C.O.'s inspection.	
		9 am	Coy. marched off to Tilth, part in practice attack.	

Army Form C. 2118.

WAR DIARY
or
INTELLIGENCE SUMMARY.
(Erase heading not required.)

Place	Date	Hour	Summary of Events and Information	Remarks and references to Appendices
RECQUES.	12/4/17	6.30 a.m	Preparing guns & limbers	
		8 a.m	Coy paraded ready for march off. Stable Parade & an attack exercise in the afternoon order.	
	13/4/17	6.30-7.30 a.m	Event ching	
		9 a.m	Range - mission	O. of inspection.
	14/4/17		Coy paraded ready to march off at 9.30 am to take part in an attack exercise in fire direction order.	
			In the afternoon preparation - rehearsal for next to WIZERNES on the 15th. 1st stage of march from to LOURE AREA.	
	15/4/17		Company march off at 10 a.m. to WIZERNES via NORDAUSQUES - ST MARTIN-AU-LAERT and outskirts of S.T OMER. Halted at TILQUES	
			for dinner and arrived WIZERNES at 3.30 pm. behaved very well on the road very nearly all day. Health very good.	
			No casualties on the march.	
NIZERNES	16/4/17		Left WIZERNES for HAZEBROUCK 7.30 am. Marched via WESTOVE - ARQUES - RENESCURE - WALLON CHAPEL - HAZEBROUCK.	

Army Form C. 2118.

WAR DIARY
or
INTELLIGENCE SUMMARY.
(Erase heading not required.)

Place	Date	Hour	Summary of Events and Information	Remarks and references to Appendices
HAZEBROUCK	16/7/17		Passed Brigadier at RENESCURE. Staff entrained WARLON CHAPEL for dinner. Arrived HAZEBROUCK at 3.0pm. Much little weather. Lorries all day but started to rain as we entered Billets. Reconnoitred Billet Area.	
BRULOOZE	17/7/17		Left HAZEBROUCK by march via PRADELLES - BAILLEUL - LOCRE - Billets KLONDYKE & FM. Rotten day rained and hailed most of the way. Fortunately cleared up as we marched through BAILLEUL. Passed GENERAL GODLEY G.O.C. ANZAC CORPS. G.O.C. 16th Div. and Brigadier General Ramsey D.S.O. latest our N.P. Slack all the way he placed them at the march past. Horses & equipment looked good as the General was pleased. PTE LLOYD was kicked down by a mule lorry on the march but was sent away to hosp. Lots of traffic the area of BAILLEUL. Arrived KLONDYKE Fm. 2.30pm	
2.8.Sw. 3a.	18/7/17		VIERSTRAAT Sector reconnoitred. Preparations handed of 47 M.G. Coy torrow.	
PIONEER FM.	19/7/17		Relieved 47 M.G. Coy. Disposition of Coy as follows.	
N.15.a.5.			Headquarters PIONEER FM. N.15.a.05. Sections at BRULOOZE N.2.d. 4.7.	

T2134. Wt. W708-776. 50C000. 4/15. Sir J.C. & S.

WAR DIARY
or
INTELLIGENCE SUMMARY.
(Erase heading not required.)

Army Form C. 2118.

Place	Date	Hour	Summary of Events and Information	Remarks and references to Appendices
PIONEER FARM.	19.7.17		Remainder of Coy arrives. Coy Operation Order No 16	APP.
	19.7.17 1.30		Indirect fire harassing carried out each night on the following targets. UNNAMED WOOD, WYTSCHAETE WOOD, PETIT BOIS, HOLLANDSCHESCHUR Salient, MAEDELSTEDE Fm, NANCY Support, 25,000 rounds have been fired.	Trench Map WYTSCHAETE 28 SW. Ed 5C.
	23/7/7		D¹ Section relieved C Section in the VANKEEP and BEYERIE positions.	
	23/7/17		'C' Section relieving E H.Q. Batln has informed us it must garrison both guns during the period includes a new I.F. Position at M.G.8. (ROSSIGNOL WOOD). Staying 3 Anti-aircraft positions. Guns I.F. Position at BESINET Farm, firing two covered dug-outs at GOSSE and PARROT Trench N.16d.9570 N.16d.9570	
	23/7/17		Indirect fire during the period. 29,500 rounds on the following points.	
	27/7/17		Light Railway WYTSCHAETE WOOD, UNNAMED WOOD and Sunken Road O.19.C. HOLLANDBCHESCHUR Salient, HOSPICE, WAR RESERVE.	
	27/7/17		Relief was carried out. L' clay. E' Section relieved 'A' Section in positions at N.22.d.4.3. N.22.d.45.55. (FORT SASKATCHEWAN) N.23 a. 2.2. (Ft CALGARY and N.22.a.9.6. (ROSSIGNOL WOOD)	

Army Form C. 2118.

WAR DIARY
or
INTELLIGENCE SUMMARY.
(Erase heading not required.)

Place	Date	Hour	Summary of Events and Information	Remarks and references to Appendices
PIONEER Pm 29.7.17	31.7.17		"J" Section relieved "B" Section in positions at N.17.a.5.7 (PARROT Fm); N.16.d.95.70 (FOSSE Fm); N.16.d.55.45 (VESINET Fm) and N.17.a.7.1. (Fm HALIFAX) "B" Section relieved "J" Section in positions YANKEER N.16.c.1.5. BRYKERIG N.17.b.3.5. and HURLEY N.17.b.10.25. (On right hand BRYKERIG position which has been moved forward slightly, HURLEY is a little further with covered dugout.) Indirect fire undertaken of ammunition 17750 rounds. Targets engaged include UNNAMED WOOD, PET 17 Bos, NANCY Support (N.12.b.) NAIL SWITCH (N.16.d) NAIL Row (N.18.b.) NAIL Support (N.18.b.) Sunken Road (O.13.c.) and WYTSCHAETE WOOD. Weather appears to have settled into a fine spell. It is quite hot in but at times unbearably so. The enemy has shelled KEMMEL and battery positions around there on several occasions. The quantity of work going on under his arm on which he takes practically no notice is extraordinary.	Front Line WYTSCHAETE 28.S.E. Ed. 5.G.

C.A.Roberts Capt
F.U.F.M.G.Coy

N° 48 COY. M.G.C.

SECRET.   OPERATION ORDER N° 16.

1. N° 48 M.G. Coy will relieve N° 47 M.G. Coy in the VIERSTRAAT sector on the 19th April 1917.

2. Disposition of the company will be as follows.

"A" section :— FORT SASKATCHEWAN (2 guns) FORT CALGARY and THE MOUND.

"B" section :— DE NET FARM — THE FOSSE — PARROT TRENCH — FORT HALIFAX.

"C" section :— THE BRYKERIE (2 guns) — VAN KEEP — PIONEER FARM.

"D" section   PIONEER FARM.

HEAD QUARTERS   PIONEER FARM.

3. Guides will be at KEMMEL CHATEAU at 10 am the 19th.

4. All trench stores including Belt Boxes will be taken over and receipts given. Duplicates to be sent to Coy. H.Q. by 12 NOON the 20th inst.

5. Movement will be by sections at 10 MINUTE interval commencing at 9 A.M. with "A" followed by "B" "C" "D" and H.Q.

6. Signallers will report at PIONEER FARM at 9 A.M. to take over lines.

7. Transport lines and R.M. stores will be taken over under arrangements to be made by LT. BANNISTER.

Completion of relief to be notified to Coy. H.Q. at PIONEER FARM by runner.

COPY N° 1+2   WAR DIARY
       3   OFFICE
       4   2nd IN COMMAND
       5   O.C. A SECTION
       6   " B "
       7   " C "
       8.   " D "
       9   SIGN: CORP:

C.R. Roberts
CAPT:
COMD. 48 M.G. COY.

WAR   DIARY:
----------oOo----------

VOLUME:- 14

FOR MONTH OF MAY, 1917.

UNIT:- 118th Machine Gun Company

Vol 13

Army Form C. 2118.

WAR DIARY
or
INTELLIGENCE SUMMARY.
(Erase heading not required.)

Instructions regarding War Diaries and Intelligence Summaries are contained in F. S. Regs., Part II. and the Staff Manual respectively. Title pages will be prepared in manuscript.

Place	Date	Hour	Summary of Events and Information	Remarks and references to Appendices
PIONEER FARM	1/5/17		Indirect fire was carried out last night. 1000 rounds on NAIL ROW, 1000 on NANCY DRIVE, 1500 on NANCY SUPPORT, 1000 on NANCY SWITCH, 1000 on NAIL ditto. Enemy shelled KEMMEL.	
	2/5/17		Usual indirect fire 7000 rounds in all were fired on Communication & Support trenches. The night was quiet.	
	3/5/17		At 10 p.m. last night gas alarm was sounded on the distance on our left. A false alarm. 5750 rounds were fired on enemy trenches & roads.	
	4/5/17		Day & night were quiet. 7000 rounds were fired during the night.	
	5/5/17		48 M.G. Coy was relieved by 47 M.G. Coy. Relief was completed at 11.30 p.m. Enemy shelled Bronn Farm in the evening without fire to R.E. Dump. 48 M.G. Coy moved into KLONDIKE FARM. Transport moved into stables nearest to KLONDIKE FARM.	

Army Form C. 2118.

WAR DIARY
or
INTELLIGENCE SUMMARY.
(Erase heading not required.)

Instructions regarding War Diaries and Intelligence Summaries are contained in F. S. Regs., Part II. and the Staff Manual respectively. Title pages will be prepared in manuscript.

Place	Date	Hour	Summary of Events and Information	Remarks and references to Appendices
KLONDIKE FARM.	6/5/17		Church Parade at Cinema Hall, LOCRE and Y.M.C.A Hut LOCRE. Sorting and cleaning of all guns and equipment.	
"	7/5/17	6.30 – 7.30 a.m. 9 a.m – 1 p.m.	Cleaning Equipment and inspection. Sorting and cleaning of Gun equipment. A fine day.	
"	8/5/17	6.30 – 7.30 a.m.	Cleaning equipment and C.O's inspection. A wet day. Carried on with cleaning guns etc in Gollati. Am required drill and fitting carburetors to box sidecars. Gun officer demonstrated the use of gun trays for horses & mules.	
"	9/5/17	7.30 a.m. 9 – 12.30 p.m.	C.O's inspection at 7.30 a.m. Route march via DRANOUTRE on BAILLEUL & LOCRE Road through CLAPP CAMP back to Coy H.Q.	

WAR DIARY
or
INTELLIGENCE SUMMARY.
(Erase heading not required.)

Army Form C. 2118.

Place	Date	Hour	Summary of Events and Information	Remarks and references to Appendices
KLONDIKE FARM.	10/5/17		6.30 – 7.30 a.m. Cleaning equipment & inspection. 9 a.m. – 10 a.m. A Section Musketry. B, C and D Sections Signalling. All Sections received instruction in fourteen German guns during the day.	
"	11/5/17		B Section on Range with two guns. Paraded at 8.30 a.m. C Section 9 a.m. – 11 a.m. Rewther Range. 11.30 a.m. – 1 p.m. German gun. D Section 9 a.m. – 10.30 a.m. German gun. 11 a.m. – 1 p.m. Rewther Range. Hot & fine weather continued.	
"	12/5/17		8.30 a.m. D Section paraded with two guns for range. 9 a.m. – 1 p.m. B & C Sections Rewther range and German gun. Church parade. C Section with two guns on range 2 – 4 p.m.	

Army Form C. 2118.

WAR DIARY
or
INTELLIGENCE SUMMARY.
(Erase heading not required.)

Instructions regarding War Diaries and Intelligence Summaries are contained in F. S. Regs., Part II. and the Staff Manual respectively. Title pages will be prepared in manuscript.

Place	Date	Hour	Summary of Events and Information	Remarks and references to Appendices
KLONDIKE FARM.	14/5/17		9 am. A Section with two guns on range. 9 am to 1 pm. C & D Sections. Revolver range and at disposal of Section Officers. 10.45 am "B" Section - 9 men from transport for innoculation; 3 O.R. Young joined the Company and taken on strength.	
"	15/5/17	8.30 am	"C" Section with two guns for Range.	
"	16/5/17	8.30 am	"D" Section with two guns for Range. All available men Paraded at 10.45 am for another Range. A Section at 10.30 am paraded for 2nd innoculation.	
"	17/5/17		Sections placed at disposal of Section Officers. Prepare for relief of 49 M.G. Coy. in the Voormezeele Sector	
"	18/5/17		49 M.G. Coy relieved by 48 M.G. Coy in the Voormezeele Sector Relief Completed by 12 noon	

Army Form C. 2118.

WAR DIARY
or
INTELLIGENCE SUMMARY.
(Erase heading not required.)

Place	Date	Hour	Summary of Events and Information	Remarks and references to Appendices
VIERSTRAAT Sector	19/5/17		Indirect fire was carried out during the night. 5500 rounds were fired on 2 on planes brought down an enemy balloon at about P.30 (aw.)	
	20/5/17		7500 rounds were fired during the night on Out wire, Communication Trenches, roads.	
	21/5/17		9000 rounds were fired during the night to cut wire, Transways. 250 rounds were fired at enemy aeroplane. Some shelling of Van Kup. All spare men working at Splinter proofs.	
	22/5/17		6000 rounds were fired during the night. Firing ceased down after 1.30 am. Fire was directed on forward dumps, roads, cut wire and communication Trenches.	
	23/5/17		2750 rounds were fired on usual targets S.P.13 and VAN KEEP were heavily shelled at intervals.	

WAR DIARY
or
INTELLIGENCE SUMMARY.

Army Form C. 2118.

Place	Date	Hour	Summary of Events and Information	Remarks and references to Appendices
VIERSTRAAT SECTOR	24/5/17		Indirect fire was carried out during the night on dumps, cut wires, and Communication Trenches. Night passed quietly. Work on "Splinter proofs" continues.	
	25/5/17		11000 rounds were fired during the night on hostile and rear targets. 10.30 pm – 11 pm rapid fire was directed on ground in rear of MAGDELSTEDE FARM & cross roads, pt S of.	
"	26/5/17		9250 rounds were fired on rear Targets and Cut wires. Work continues on Splinter proofs.	
"	27/5/17		14000 rounds were fired during the night on cut wire, work, dumps and Communication Trenches. A.A. machine gun fired on Kite Balloon at BYRON FARM.	
"	29/5/17		48750 rounds were fired during the month and for research firing etc.	

WAR DIARY
or
INTELLIGENCE SUMMARY.
(Erase heading not required.)

Army Form C. 2118.

Place	Date	Hour	Summary of Events and Information	Remarks and references to Appendices
VIERSTRAAT SECTOR.	29/5/17		Indiscriminate fire was carried out last night. 13500 rounds being fired on cut wire. Bois de WYTSCHAETE, roads, dumps and communication trenches. Enemy shelled WATLING STREET and into YORK ROAD. ROSSIGNOL WOOD was also shelled and FORT HALIFAX. Shells fell in the vicinity of Beaver and PIONEER FARMS.	
"	30/5/17		9000 rounds were fired last night on cut wire and communication trenches & roads. ROSSIGNOL WOOD was shelled at 9.45 p.m. Battery positions between PG FARM and YORK Rd were shelled. At about 1.00 am the enemy was seen & trench lijht.	
"	31/5/17		Indiscriminate fire was carried out during the night. 9750 rounds being fired. Enemy shelled HALIFAX at 3 a.m. Roslwinj & and surrounding. 3 of the guns team. Work was continued on gun emplacements.	

C.W. Roberts Capt.
O.C. 4th Machine Gun Coy.

Secret   48 COY. M.G.C.   Copy No 2

OPERATION ORDER No 23.   17-5-17

1. No 48 M.G.Coy will relieve 49 MG Coy in the VIERSTRAAT SECTOR on the 18TH MAY 1917.
   Relief to be complete by 12 NOON.

2. Disposition of company will be as follows
   "A" SECTION ------------------ PIONEER FARM.
   B   "   , SP12 – VAN KEEP – FT. SASKATCHEWAN (2 Guns)
   C   "   , FOSSE – PARROT TRENCH – BRYKERIE – HURLEY.
   D   "   , MOUND – FT CALGARY – FT. HALIFAX – DESINET.
   HEAD QRS. ------- PIONEER FARM

3. One guide will be at KEMMEL CHATEAU for SP12 positions at 8 AM.

4. All trench stores and barrack stores, except belt boxes will be taken over and receipts given. Duplicates to be sent to Coy. HQ by 12 NOON the 19TH inst.

5. Route:– BUTTERFLY FM. – AU.POMPIER ESTAMINET – KEMMEL.
   Movement will be by sections at 10 minute interval, commencing at 7 AM with "A" Section followed by "B. C. D & H.Q.

6. Signallers will report to PIONEER FM at 9 AM and take over line

7. 2M stores will be taken to PIONEER FM.
   All gun equipment not required in the trenches will be stored at PIONEER FM except S.A.A. which will be taken to transport lines.
   Two limbers with 120 belt boxes will reach the "MOUND" at 3.30 AM and dump the boxes there. An N.C.O and two men from "A" section will go with the limbers, unload them and guard the dump until the gun team take over the boxes.

8. Completion of relief to be notified to COY. H.Q at PIONEER FARM by runner

                                         K.H.Bannister, LT
                                         48 M.G. COY

COPIES TO:–
     Nos 1 + 2   WAR DIARY   No 7   OC. "C" SECTION
          3   "   OFFICE   8   "   D   "
          4   TP. OFFICER   9   SIGNAL CPL
          5   OC "A" SECTION
          6   "   B   "

N° 48 MACHINE GUN COY.
OPERATION ORDER N° 22.

Ref. M 22 S.W. 1/20.000.   4-5-17

1. N° 48 M.G.Coy will be relieved by N° 47 M.G.Coy in VIERSTRAAT section on May 5th 1917.

2. One guide per gun will be detailed from A.2 to meet relieving teams of 47 M.G.Coy at CHATEAU KEMMEL at 10 A.M.

3. Trench stores and trench stores will be handed over and receipts obtained. Boots gum thigh and 10 Belt Boxes per gun will be treated as trench stores. Certificate will be prepared at each gun position as well as total list prepared at Section H.Q.

4. A carrying party of one man per gun will report to Section H.Q. at 9.30 a.m. Guides will act as additional carriers.

5. Transport will await relieved teams in KEMMEL from 11 A.M.

6. On completion of relief, sections will proceed to KLONDYKE FARM.

7. <u>Relief of PIONEER F.M. & TRANSPORT LINES.</u>
   (A) Reserve guns, equipment, blankets, packs and all kit, to be stacked outside the O.R. by 8 A.M.
   (B) 2nd Lt. D. EDWARDS will proceed in advance to KLONDYKE F.M. and take over trench stores and belt Boxes.
   (C) 2nd Lt. A.M. ADAIR will hand over PIONEER F.M.
   (D) All parties to be clear of PIONEER F.M. by 10 A.M.
   (E) Transport lines will be handed over under arrangements to be made by Lt. R.H. BANNISTER.

COPIES TO: N° 1 & 2. WAR DIARY   J.E. Gatehly Lt.
          " 3.   2nd I/C.   48 M.G. COY.
          " 4   O.C. A. SECTION
          " 5   " B "
          " 6   " D "
          " 7   O. MESS.

WAR DIARY.

FOR MONTH OF JUNE, 1917.

VOLUME:- 15

UNIT:- 48th Machine Gun Company

Army Form C. 2118.

WAR DIARY
or
INTELLIGENCE SUMMARY.

(Erase heading not required.)

175th Machine Gun Company

Place	Date	Hour	Summary of Events and Information	Remarks and references to Appendices
VIERSTRAAT SECTOR	1/6/17		H.Q. at PIONEER FARM. Work on splinter-proof shelters at BRYKERIF finished. Sergeant TAYLOR admitted to hospital.	
	2/6/17		Manuscript 2nd/3rd 48 M.G.Coy relieved by 47 & 49 M.G.Coys in VIERSTRAAT SECTOR. Shelling during relief.	
CLARE CAMP	3/6/17		The Company moved to CLARE CAMP from PIONEER FARM & remained. Relief completed by 6 a.m. Lines changed at CLARE CAMP during the day.	
	4/6/17		General cleaning up of guns & personnel. Camp shelled during the afternoon.	
	5/6/17		No shelling. More cleaning up.	
	6/6/17		CLARE CAMP shelled during the morning. Preparations made for the trenches. Company left CLARE CAMP about 10 p.m. for the trenches.	
	7/6/17 2:30am		All guns in position to M.G. barrage for attack on MYTSCHAETE RIDGE. viz. FORT HALIFAX & guns, BRVKERIE 4 guns, POTROT TRENCH 4 guns. Company H.Q. – La FOSSE.	

Army Form C. 2118.

WAR DIARY
or
INTELLIGENCE SUMMARY.
(Erase heading not required.)

Instructions regarding War Diaries and Intelligence Summaries are contained in F. S. Regs., Part II. and the Staff Manual respectively. Title pages will be prepared in manuscript.

Place	Date	Hour	Summary of Events and Information	Remarks and references to Appendices
VIERSTRAAT SECTOR.	7/6/17	3.10 a.m.	Zero hour. All guns open barrage & continue till 6.50 a.m. 18,000 rounds fired. After this all guns assembled at FORT HALIFAX and St. Walker. 2nd Lieuts. Edwards, Young, Dawson took two guns each to report to battalion.	
		11.7 a.m.	Remaining guns with Capt. Roberts and Lt. Kirkland & 2nd Lieut. Adair move off to take up positions in MAUVEZINE. These guns in position by 3.30 p.m. night quiet. Enemy artillery active during the afternoon - enemy towards dusk. All guns replied to our SOS shortly after dusk firing about 2500 rounds per gun.	
	9/6/17		Day quiet. Company relieved by 34 M.G. Coy about 10.30 p.m. & move to FORT HALIFAX. Shelling during relief.	
	10/6/17	3 a.m.	Relief completed. Total casualties for June 7th, 8th, 9th, 10th. Rate of Wounds - 1 O.R. wounded - 7 O.R. 1 officer. One gun destroyed during relief. Capt. Rand proceeded to S/SA GHQ.	
	11/6/17		Belt-Boxes fetched from 34 M.G. Coy. 48 m.t. Coy move to	

Army Form C. 2118.

WAR DIARY
or
INTELLIGENCE SUMMARY.
(Erase heading not required.)

Place	Date	Hour	Summary of Events and Information	Remarks and references to Appendices
CLARE CAMP	11/6/17		CLARE CAMP. During the evening move to small camp some distance from CLARE CAMP.	
	12/6/17		2nd Lieut. Owen and 2 guns "D" Section go on Anti-Aircraft duty at TRENT DUMP.	
STRAZEELE	13/6/17		48 M.T. Coy. move into billets at STRAZEELE.	
	14/6/17		Cleaning up & refitting company.	
	15/6/17		Inspection by O.C. C. 48th Inf. Bde.	
	16/6/17		Further cleaning up & refitting.	
	17/6/17		Company move into canvas at WESTOUTRE. Transport at CLARE CAMP.	
ST RAZEELE	18/6/17		Company move back into same billets at STRAZEELE.	
	19/6/17		Guns return from TRENT DUMP, 2nd Lieut Caldwell joins the Company.	
St SILVESTRE	20/6/17		Company marches to St. SILVESTRE - CAPPEL into billets.	
CAPPEL	21/6/17		Cleaning up under Section Officers.	

Army Form C. 2118.

WAR DIARY
or
INTELLIGENCE SUMMARY.
(Erase heading not required.)

Place	Date	Hour	Summary of Events and Information	Remarks and references to Appendices
RUBROUCK	22/6/17		48th M.G. Coy moves into billets in RUBROUCK area & march past 2nd Army Commander.	
	23/6/17		Cleaning up - drill under section officers.	
	24/6/17		Sunday. Church parade at RUBROUCK BRASSERIE.	
	25/6/17		Capt C.L. Roberts returns to England. Company inspected by G.O.C. 145th Inf. Bde.	
	26/6/17		Second inspection by G.O.C.	
	27/6/17		Company inspected by Corps Commander & congratulated by G.O.C. 16th Division. Training under section officers.	
	28/6/17		Training continued. Capt Rando arrives back from M.G. School, and assumed command of Company.	
	29/6/17			
	30/6/17		Further training. Limber - Drill - Night march.	

E.W. Wallace Lt.
for Capt.
O.C. 48th Machine Gun Company

APPENDIX I

SECRET   OPERATION ORDER Nº 26   COPY Nº 2

48 MACHINE GUN COY

1. Nº 48 Machine Gun Company will be relieved in VIERSTRAAT SECTOR by Nºs 47 & 49 Machine Gun Companies on the night 2/3rd JUNE 1917.

2. (a) Nº 47 Machine Gun Company will take over the following positions:-
THE MOUND, FORT HALIFAX, S.P. 12, CALGARY
and 2 GUNS in FORT SASKATCHEWAN

(b) Nº 49 Machine Gun Company will take over positions
DESINET FARM, THE FOSSE, PARROT TRENCH
BRYKERIE, HURLEY & VAN KEEP and billets at
PIONEER FARM.

3. Guides for 47 Machine Gun Company will be detailed from Head-
Quarters to meet relieving teams at the CHATEAU KEMMEL
at 11.30 P.M.

No guides will be detailed for 49 Machine Gun Company, but
relieving teams will leave billets at KLONDYKE F.M. at 9 P.M.

Trench stores will be handed over on all site to takes effect throughout. A carrying party from HEADQUARTERS will be detailed
to assist relieved teams.

4. Limbers will wait for Sections on YORK RD, as follows:-

    D SECTION ------- DOCTORS HOUSE
    A   "   ------- THE MOUND
    B   "   ------- THE FOSSE

5. On completion of relief Sections will proceed to camp at CLARE
CAMP and will keep as far as possible to cross country tracks.
A Billeting party consisting of 1 NCO and 5 men under Lt F.
KIRKLAND will report to CLARE CAMP by 6 P.M. 2-6-17

Copies to 1 & 2 WAR DIARY
    3 - O.C. Company   R.W. Bannister Lt
    4 - 2nd I/C.   48. M.G. Coy.
    5 - O.C. A Section
    6 - " B "
    7 - " C "
    8 - " D "
    9 - " Transport
   10 - Capt RANDS

SECRET.   APPENDIX II

                                                                    16

MAP [illegible]

(a) [illegible] part of [illegible] by the SECOND [illegible]
(b) [illegible] simultaneously on the right and the [illegible] Division [illegible]
(c) The Seventh Division [illegible] Brigade [illegible] in reserve.

    18TH BTN.   7 INFANTRY BRIGADE with 156 Coy R.E.
                      one company 11TH HANTS &

    [illegible]   [illegible] with 157 Coy
                      R.E, one company 11TH HANTS alt

    IN RESERVE   48TH [illegible] with [illegible] Coy
                      TWO companies 11TH [illegible]

(d) The supporting attached to the DIVISION [illegible]
    map have been [illegible] to the [illegible]
        1st OBJECTIVE   RED
        2nd OBJECTIVE   BLUE
        3rd OBJECTIVE   GREEN
        [illegible] OBJECTIVE   [illegible]
        [illegible] OBJECTIVE   [illegible]

    Boundaries between Divisions are shown in [illegible]
    [illegible] IMPORTANT [illegible]
    RED.

    [illegible] the times of arrival and departure
    [illegible]
    RED LINE   ARRIVE 0.5[?]
                      [illegible]
    BLUE LINE   ARRIVE 1.10
                      DEPART [illegible]
    GREEN LINE   ARRIVE 4.10
                      DEPART 6.20

SHEET 2

BLACK LINE ...... ARRIVE ZERO + 4.40
MAUVE LINE ...... ARRIVE ZERO + 6.30

With the exception of GREEN LINE, all lines will be
consolidated after capture.
All C.O's will make themselves acquainted with this map.

Dispositions immediately prior to attack:-
Reserve Infantry Brigade HQ ..... THE FOSSE
BATTALIONS .... One Battalion in CHINESE WALL LINE
  NORTH OF ROSIGNOL RD. H.Q. S.P.
  ONE Battalion in CHINESE WALL
  Line SOUTH of ROSIGNOL RD. H.Q
  IRISH HOUSE dug out.
  One Battalion on VIERSTRAAT
  SWITCH, NORTH OF DESINET FARM
  H.Q THE FOSSE.
  ONE BATTALION VIERSTRAAT
  SWITCH, SOUTH OF DESINET FARM
  H.Q THE FOSSE
  L$ M.G.COY HQ THE FOSSE (N.16 b.5.5)
  L$ T.M. Battery FORT MOUNT ROYAL -
  FORT CALGARY

EMPLOYMENT OF MACHINE GUNS FOR COVERING AND BARRAGE FIRE
The machine guns are allotted for covering and barrage
fire and are divided into three categories.
(a) Guns to establish a creeping barrage either direct,
    enfilade or oblique, in front of the Artillery barrage.
    The object of this barrage is to catch the enemy suspic-
    ious.. from the heavies or sheltering in shell holes
    or ditches between the guns.
(b) Guns detailed for fire on selected targets, such as
    strong points, cuttings or ravines.
    Guns to sweep all ground in front and rear of the
    enemy's machine of resistance from the close of one
    of the attack. All guns will be given a definite task or
    line in order to cover the pauses at the
    ...... objectives.

SHEET 2.

EMPLOYMENT OF MACHINE GUNS WITH ASSAULTING BATTALIONS.

(a) Guns allotted to assaulting infantry battalions will work in pairs, each pair under an officer, and in each case will accompany the final wave.

(b) The tasks for which they are to be used during the attack are:-
   1. To protect the assaulting battalions against counter attacks during the assault.
   2. After the capture of the MAUVE LINE to assist the consolidation by taking up positions to cover the ground in front of these lines.
   3. To take advantage of good fleeting targets in order to inflict loss on the enemy.
   4. To cover the front of any gap which may occur in our lines.

(c) As soon as the battalions reach their objectives and halting places, every effort must be made to get forward an adequate supply of ammunition for these guns by means of carrying parties and pack mules.

Barrage zones of fire have been allotted by IX CORPS to the various attacking divisions. The zone allotted to 16th DIVISION is as follows:-

From line NAP DRIVE (inclusive) – HILL 84 (inclusive) – STEENYZER CABARET (inclusive).

To line: RED CHATEAU – junction of OBVIOUS AVENUE with OBVIOUS ROW – house C.14.C.30.50.

SPECIAL.

The allocation of zones to the 48th INF. BDE GROUP is the 48th M.
G. Coy guns (less 4 at PARROT FM.) which will search from the
line separating squares N and O between the RED CHATEAU and
NANCY DRIVE forward to the 100x E. of a NORTH and SOUTH line
through O.13. Central and O.19 Central. When the advance from
the RED LINE begins at ZERO + 1 hour 5 minutes, they will creep
forward to a N and S line through NORTH HO. from OBSTRUC-
TION DRIVE on the N. to the WYTSCHAETE - TORREKEN FARM
ROAD on the S. On the advance from the BLUE LINE at ZERO
+ 3hr. 40 mins. they will creep forward until out of range.
They will then concentrate at FORT HALIFAX.

The four guns at PARROT FM. will at ZERO begin searching from
front of PETIT BOIS through BOIS DE WYTSCHAETE. They
will eventually creep their barrage forward to the centre of
WYTSCHAETE and cease when the advance from the BLUE
LINE begins at ZERO + 3hrs 40 mins. They will then
concentrate at FORT HALIFAX.

The grouping of guns for barrage zones will be as follows :-

FORT HALIFAX

2 Guns A Section under 2nd LT. D. EDWARDS.
2 "   B   "   "   LT. J.E. GATELY.
2 "   C   "   "   LT. E.W. WALLACE
2 "   D   "   "   2nd LT. PAH OSWIN

Fire will be controlled by LT J.E. GATELY.

DRYKERIE

2 Guns C Section under LT F. KIRKLAND.
2 "   D   "   "   2nd LT T.W. YOUNG.

Fire will be controlled by LT F. KIRKLAND.

PARROT TRENCH

2 Guns A Section) under 2nd LT A. DAIR.
2 "   B   "   )

3. Guns are allotted to Battalions of the 48th INF Brigade on the MAUVE LINE as follows:

   2 Guns "A" section under 2nd Lt. EDWARDS   9th R. DUBLINS.
   2 Guns "B" section under Lieut. GATELY   8th R. DUBLINS.
   2 Guns "C" section under Lieut. WALLACE   7th R. I. RIFLES.
   2 Guns "D" section under 2nd Lt. OSWALD   2nd R.D.F.

4. After concentration at FORT HALIFAX the remaining 8 guns will move forward and occupy the MAUVE LINE about the RAILWAY approx. at O.21.c.60.10 immediately the 33RD BDE have passed through at ZERO + 10 hrs. (NEW ZERO).

They will put up a protective barrage from the year zero at O.23.a.10.20 to O.28.c.30.20. They will fire on this Line in reply to S.O.S. when one or two guns will be employed to sear a road alongside the new front of about 4 to 800 yds. East of this final Line. After NEW ZERO + 1 hour (or Zero + 11 hours) they will be no M.G. fire except in reply to S.O.S.

5. After OLD ZERO + 4 hours the main M.G. dump for ammunition etc. will be FORT HALIFAX. As soon as possible after the 33RD BDE have passed through the Mauve Line at ZERO + 10 hours (NEW ZERO) this dump will be advanced by means of pack transport to the vicinity of SCHENZER CAB O.20.c.

6. The S.O.S. will be a single RED VERY LIGHT.

7. Z day and ZERO hour will be communicated later.

C. P. Roberts
Capt.

Comdg 48 M.G. Coy.

Secret. APPENDIX III Copy No. 3

No. 48 Coy. Machine Gun Corps.
Operation Order No.

Map Reference Sheet 27/40,000.   21st June 1917

1. No 48 Machine Gun Coy will move to billets in the RUBROUCK Training area on June 22nd in accordance with 48th Infantry Brigade Order No 129 dated 21st June 17.

2. Route will be – Road Junction P.10.a.2.4. – HAEGDEONE (J.31.b) – Road Junction I.36.C.2.0 – CROIX ROUGE – L'ANGE – ARNEKE – Billets.
Head of column to pass starting point P.10.a.2.4 at 5.40 am

3. A Billetting party consisting of Lt. F. KIRKLAND and 2. O.R. will proceed in advance and report to the Staff Capt. at the Church ST SYLVESTRE CHAPEL by 3 pm. 21st inst.

4. All transport will be packed by 4.15 am on 22nd inst.

5. Company parade in fighting order at the Transport Lines. March off 4.45 am.

6. 2nd Lt. D. EDWARDS will ride ahead of the Company at a sufficient distance to give warning to the Traffic Control posts of the approach of the Column.

Copy No 1 Fitt
        2. 3. War Diary
        4. Officers Mess

C. H. Roberts
Capt.
O.C. 48. M. Gun Coy.

WAR DIARY.

FOR MONTH OF JULY, 1917.

VOLUME :- 16

UNIT :- 48th Machine Gun Coy

Army Form C. 2118.

WAR DIARY
or
INTELLIGENCE SUMMARY.
(Erase heading not required.)

Instructions regarding War Diaries and Intelligence Summaries are contained in F. S. Regs., Part II. and the Staff Manual respectively. Title pages will be prepared in manuscript.

Place	Date	Hour	Summary of Events and Information	Remarks and references to Appendices
RUBROUCK	1.7.17		Company musketry. Company training carried out under	
	2.7.17		Company arrangements	
	3.7.17		Company training bath.	
	4.7.17		Company training	
	5.7.17		Company training. Strength 1 bury. Off 9. O.R. 162	
	6.7.17		Company training	
	7.7.17		Church Parade	
	8.7.17		Company moved into billets in TATINGHEM area in accordance with 48 BRIGADE operation order No 131 dated	APPENDIX 1
TATINGHEM	9.7.17		7.7.17. Raining most of the way. Billets quite good. Company training	
	10.7.17		Company training. 32 O.R. attached to Company from Infantry	
	11.7.17		Brigade tactical scheme	
	12.7.17		Company tactical scheme	
	13.7.17		Brigade tactical scheme	

Army Form C. 2118.

WAR DIARY
or
INTELLIGENCE SUMMARY.
(Erase heading not required.)

Instructions regarding War Diaries and Intelligence Summaries are contained in F. S. Regs., Part II. and the Staff Manual respectively. Title pages will be prepared in manuscript.

Place	Date	Hour	Summary of Events and Information	Remarks and references to Appendices
TATINGHEM	14.7.17		Brigade tactical scheme. Inspection of Brigade during manoeuvres by Divisional General. Very wet.	
	15.7.17		Church parade. 2/Lt. CATCHPOLE & 3 W. 2/Lt. EGGLETON joined Company and taken on the strength. Strength of Company OFF. 11 OR. 163. attached O.R. 32.	
ERINGHAM Area	16.7.17		Company moved into billets in ERINGHAM area in accordance with Brigade of operation orders No 133, dated 15.7.17. The men fell out during the march.	APPENDIX 2
map ref. 1.29 a.4.9. 9 ref. 19.	17.7.17		Company training.	
	18.7.17		Company parade cleaning etc. @ 3 O.R. reported arrival and taken on strength. Strength of Coy. OFF. 11. OR. 167. att O.R. 32	
	19.7.17		Company inspected by Army Commander. Praised for smartness of turn out. 12 O.R. reported arrival and taken on strength. Strength of Company OFF. 11, OR 179, att O.R. 32. General health of Company very good. Men very cheerful & content	

Army Form C. 2118.

WAR DIARY
or
INTELLIGENCE SUMMARY.
(Erase heading not required.)

Instructions regarding War Diaries and Intelligence Summaries are contained in F.S. Regs., Part II. and the Staff Manual respectively. Title pages will be prepared in manuscript.

Place	Date	Hour	Summary of Events and Information	Remarks and references to Appendices
ERINGHAM area T29.a.H.9 Sht 19	20.7.17		Company training. Nothing of importance happened in the company during the last few days. 14 O.R. reported arrival from H.Q. M.G. Coy. Taken on strength accordingly. Strength of Company OFF. 11. O.R. 193. OR attached 32.	Stores
	21.7.17		Company training. Nothing of any importance happened. Men lectured on the importance of precaution against gas. Helmets (Box) inspected by Coy. Gas Officer.	Coy.
WINNEZEELE area M.3 I.12.d.4.7 map B.f.	22.7.17		Company moved into billets in WINNEZEELE area No 3 in accordance with 48th Infantry Brigade Operation Order No.134. dated 19.7.17. 1 O.R. injured in the face by a kick from an officers charger, the boy was taken at the line. Billets and transport lines quite good. Weather fine, very warm.	APPENDIX 3
	23.7.17		Company training. Reconnaissance of line near YPRES by Lt WALLACE. 2/Lt COLDWELL 2/Lt GATCHPOLE left billets at 9 A.M. returned 5.30 P.M. 2 O.R. evacuated and struck off the strength. Strength of Coy OFF. 11. O.R. 191. OR attached 32.	Bath

WAR DIARY
or
INTELLIGENCE SUMMARY.
(Erase heading not required.)

Army Form C. 2118.

Place	Date	Hour	Summary of Events and Information	Remarks and references to Appendices
WINNEZEELE area map ref. Index 7.	24.7.17.		Company training. Parade at 4 Bde H.Q. firing out of ribbons for honours won. Pte M°CARTE of this Coy received the M.M. Ribbon. Divisional Certificates received for Capt C.L. ROBERTS, Sgt PETTIGREW and Pte M°CARTE of this Coy. Nothing unusual occurred. 5 O.R. sent to CAMIERS (MACHINE GUN BASE DEPOT) who was no machine Gunners. Strength of Coy OFF 11. O.R. 186 attached O.R. 32.	B.W.D. B.W.D.
WATOU area map ref L.15.6.9.1.	25.7.17		Coy moved into tents in the WATOU area in accordance with 48th Infantry Brigade Operation Orders No. 135. dated 22.7.17. Very wet during the move. Tents very crowded. Transport lines quite good. 1 O.R. sent to MACHINE GUN BASE DEPOT CAMIERS as unfit for a machine gunner and struck off strength of Coy. Strength of Coy OFF 11. O.R. 185. O.R. attached 32.	APPENDIX 4 Evans
WATOU	26.7.17		Company training. Orders for the Offensive received during the past week. More training on enemy Map.	Esser
	27.7.17		Company training. Nothing unusual happened. Capt RANOS went to Conference at Brigade H.Q. to discuss coming Offensive. Maps received from Brigade. Lt ADAIR saw the model	Capt. RANOS. Evans Evans

WAR DIARY
or
INTELLIGENCE SUMMARY.
(Erase heading not required.)

Army Form C. 2118.

Place	Date	Hour	Summary of Events and Information	Remarks and references to Appendices
WATOU L15.b.91.	28.7.17	2 P.M.	Company training. Nothing unusual. Company Officers N.C.O's & the men detailed as guides saw the Model. 3 O.R. attached evacuated Sick, applied to Batt. to replace their strength of Coy. OFF. 11. O.R. 183. O.R. attached 29.	Corr. Corr.
	29.7.17.		Preparation made for coming offensive. Inspection of Gas Returns & Gas appliances. Brigade operation orders received for move to BRANDHOEK	APPENDIX 5.
	30.7.17.		Company resting all men issued with two days rations. Brigade H.Q. sent round secret message stating Zero hour for coming offensive. Then was 3.50 A.M. 31.7.17. Roads were very congested during the move to position of readiness at St Lawrence Camp. Map ref. C.11.a. 6.0.	
C.11.a.6.0.	31.7.17.		Headquarters, A. B. C & D sections with fighting numbers moved from C.11.a.6.0. at 3 A.M. to assembly position	End

WAR DIARY
or
INTELLIGENCE SUMMARY

Army Form C. 2118.

(Erase heading not required.)

Place	Date	Hour	Summary of Events and Information	Remarks and references to Appendices
C.11a.c.p.	31/7/17	3 p.m.	at H. 16.a.4.9. arrived 5 a.m. Roads very congested on way up. Everything quiet during the day. One shell lit in the same field two men of another unit injured. No casualties in the Company.	Ours
		6.30 p.m.	Message received from 4th Inf Bde. ordering the Company to be ready to move at a moments notice at 6.45 p.m the Company was ready to move off. Capt RANDS proceeded on to Brigade H.Q. returning at 7.15 p.m. with instructions that the Company would proceed to BRANDHOEK. Moved off at 8.0 p.m. arrived BRANDHOEK at 9.0 p.m. Company ready to move forward again at a moments notice.	

E. Eyre Rantor
Capt.

APPENDIX I

No. 48 Coy. M.G.C.

SECRET.   Copy No. 1

OPERATION ORDER No. 31.

Refce. HAZEBROUCK Sheet Scale 1/100,000.

In the Field
7-7-1917

(1) No. 48 Coy. M.G.C. will move to billets in the TATINGHEM area on 8-7-1917 in accordance with 48 Brigade Operation Orders No. 131 dated 7-7-1917.

(2) A billeting party consisting of Lt KIRKLAND and one signaller will proceed one hour in advance of the Company and will meet Sgt CLARK who proceeded to the area to-day to take over billets from 49 Coy. M.G.C.

(3) Company will parade, in fighting order, ready to move off by 5.45 a.m. with head of the column 200 yds. S.W. of Company Office. It will pass starting point - forked roads 400 yds S.W. of B in BROXEELE at 6.25 a.m.

(4) All transport will be packed by 5 a.m. and will form up on road leading NNW from Company Office by 5.45 a.m.

(5) Route will be RUBROUCK - BROXEELE - HALTE "S" N. ST MOMELIN - ST OMER - TATINGHEM.

(6) Every man falling out on line of march will be provided with a slip signed by an officer.

(7) The C.O. will march at the head of the Company.

E. W. Wallace Lt.
O. 48 Coy. M.G.C.

Issued at 3.45 p.m.

Copies to :-
1 & 2 War Diary.
3.   O.C.
4.   Officers' Mess.
5.   Company Office.

APPENDIX 2

SECRET.   **No. 48 Coy. M.G.C.**   Copy No. 2

OPERATION ORDERS No. 33.

Ref. Map. HAZEBROUCK 5a   In the Field.
1/100,000.   15-7-17.

① The Company will move to billets in the ERINGHAM area on Monday 16-7-17 in accordance with Brigade Operation Orders No 133 dated 15-7-17.

② The Company will parade in Fighting Order outside Company billets ready to move at 4-45 am and will pass starting point – cross roads ST MARTIN AU LAERT at 5-42 am.

③ All limbers etc to be packed by 4-15 am.

④ Transport will form up on road leading from Transport lines to 30 yds S. of Company billets with head at latter point.

⑤ All men falling out on march will be provided with a slip signed by an officer.

⑥ Strict march discipline will be enforced.

⑦ LT. KIRKLAND has proceeded to ERINGHAM area as billetting officer to-day and will meet Company at cross roads S of ERKELSBRUGG at 10-0 am 16-7-17.

⑧ The C.O. will march at the head of the Company.

E. W. Wallace LT.
Issued at 4 p.m.   No. 48 Coy. M.G.C.

Copies to :-
  1 & 2 War Diaries.
  3   C.O.
  4   2 i/c.
  5   Officers' Mess.
  6   Transport Officer.
  7   File.

APPENDIX 3

SECRET.   **No. 48 Coy. M.G.C.**   Copy No. 2

OPERATION ORDERS No. 34

Refce. HAZEBROUCK 5a.   In the Field
                                     21-VII-1917

① The 4-8th Infantry Brigade will march to the WINNEZEELE area No 3.
   The 48 Coy. M.G.C. will move on 22-7-17 to billets about ROOSENDAEL in accordance with 48th Infantry Brigade Operation Orders No 134 dated 19-7-17

② The Company will parade in fighting order at billets ready to move at 6.15 a.m. Steel helmets will be carried on haversack. Respirators will be worn.

③ The Company will pass starting point CHURCH, ZEGGERS-CAPPEL at 7.15 a.m.

④ LIEUT EDWARDS and PTE HOGG have proceeded to billeting area to-day

⑤ All transport to be packed by 6.30 a.m.

⑥ Transport will form up in line in rear of Company

⑦ All men falling out must have in their possession a "chit" signed by an officer.

Issued at 7 p.m.

                                E. Wallace LIEUT.
                                No. 48 Coy. M.G.C.

Copies to :-
   1 & 2 War Diary ✓
   3   C.O.
   4   2nd I/C.
   5   Transport Officer
   6   Officers' Mess

APPENDIX 4.

SECRET   No 48 Coy. M.G.C.   Copy No. 2

OPERATION ORDERS No 35

Refce Map - Sheet 27.   In the Field.
                                                               24.7.17.

1. The 48th Brigade will march to the WATOU No. 1 area on 25-7-1917.
No 48 Coy. M.G.C. will move to billets about L.15 b.q.1. in accordance with 48 Infantry Brigade Operation Orders No 135 dated 22.7.17.

2. Company parade in Fighting Order ready to move off at 4.45 am. Steel helmets and P.H. helmets will be carried. Box respirators will be carried as usual.

3. The Company will pass "starting point" - cross roads J.8.a.7.2. at 5.25 am.

4. Route - Cross roads J.22.c.10.0. - WINNEZEELE - WATOU ROAD JUNCTION - K.4.b.5.0 - Cross-roads K.12.c - Road Junction - L.13.d.5.0.

5. Guides will meet the Company at cross-roads at Q.12.c.

6. Lieut. EDWARDS and PTE HOGG proceeded today as billeting party.

7. All transport to be packed by 4.15 am.
Transport will be formed up in field at Company billets.

8. Strict march discipline will be enforced.

Issued at .... pm.   E.W. Wallace LT.
                              No. 48 Coy. M.G.C.

Copies to:
1 & 2   War Diary
3   C.O.
4   2nd i/c.
5   Transport Officer.
6   Officers' Mess.
7   File.

Copy No 2

APPENDIX 5.

48 Coy M.G.C.

Operation Order No 86

Sheets 27 and 28   29.7.17

1. The company will move to positions of readiness on 30-7-17 in accordance with 48 Brigade operation orders No 186-d-29 [...], and march table A attached, and thence at Zero hour to position of assembly in accordance with march table B.

2.(a) Company will parade in fighting order with packs ready to move at 8.50 PM, and will pass starting point at L.H.B.8.8 at 9.40 PM.

 b. Company will move as "Action imminent" with 200 yards distance between sections.

3. Each man will be in possession of two full days rations in addition to emergency ration, when marching out.

4.(a) All transport will accompany the company to position of readiness.

 (b) No wheeled transport will move EAST of this position except :- WATER CART, MESS CART and Nos 1 and 2 limbers.

5. An aeroplane sentry will be posted on arrival at position of assembly, and troops will be concealed from enemy observation.

6. A billeting party under 2nd Lt CATCHPOLE will precede the company to position of readiness, with Sgt. CLARKE and two cooks, and two men to be detailed by C.S.M. Time to be notified later. One No 3 limber will proceed with the party

Sheet 2.

7. Zero hour and date will be notified later
8. The C.O. will march at the head of the
   company.

       E.W. Wallace. LT
       48 Coy. M.G.C.

Issued at --------- A.M.
Copies to:-
1 and 2. War diary
  3. C.O.
  4. 2nd I/C
  5. Transport Officer.
  6. File.
  7. O.C. A Section
  8. " B "
  9. " C "
  10. " D "
  11. B.Q.M.S.
  12.

WAR DIARY.

FOR MONTH OF AUGUST, 1917.

VOLUME......17.

UNIT 48th Machine Gun Company

Army Form C. 2118.

WAR DIARY
or
INTELLIGENCE SUMMARY.

(Erase heading not required.)

48th M.G. Coy

Place	Date	Hour	Summary of Events and Information	Remarks and references to Appendices
BRANDHOEK	5/17		Company ready to move off at a moments notice. Officers went off with boats patties. Nothing of any importance during the day. The weather tried awful but officers were under shots so we were not too badly off. Still waiting for orders. The men of the men were evident awaiting fit hut conditions.	
	6/17		Enemy heavy bombardment took place during night. 1st S.D. Brough being heavily shelled. Still raining but still standing by awaiting orders. Orders were issued from 48 Inf.y Bde. Attacks w/ing Operation Orders dated 2.8-17. Therewith. In two days a tour assured to all. Guns cleaned & boilers boiled. Fair amount of ant-aircraft amongst men. So all sorts of rumours going about. Bus & airplane enemy posts. Very quiet	

WAR DIARY or INTELLIGENCE SUMMARY

Army Form C. 2118.

Place	Date	Hour	Summary of Events and Information	Remarks and references to Appendices
BRANDHOEK	3/8/17	3 AM	Capt. Roads, Lt. Adair, 2nd Lts. Oswin and Catchpole left Coy HQ. to reconnoitre positions held by 44 M.G. Coy. in front of YPRES. Positions reconnoitred & details handed over by O.C. 44 M.G. Coy. to O.C. 48 M.G. Coy. Lt. Adair & 2nd Catchpole left the line to guide A, B, & D sections into positions at B & D under Lts. Wallace, Bannister & Kirkland moved to Asylum YPRES at 2.30 p.m. and were met by Lts. Adair & Catchpole. 2nd Lt. Caldwell plus two gun teams of "A" section moved forward to front line. 2nd Lt. Catchpole i/c two gun teams of "D". Lt. Oswin i/c two guns of "D" & Lt. Adair and 2nd Lt. Eggleton i/c of the gun of "B" & 2 guns of "A" in Iben Reserve brought two C.O's HQ to Wilde Wood. Relief of 44 M.G. Coy complete at 7 p.m. Men were very tired as they had been going two days with very little sleep. The relief took place during daylight consequently all teams had a very trying time from the enemy who constantly annoying	48th M.G. Coy

Army Form C. 2118.

WAR DIARY
or
INTELLIGENCE SUMMARY.

(Erase heading not required.)

Place	Date	Hour	Summary of Events and Information	Remarks and references to Appendices
BRANDHOEK	4/9/17		C Section in reserve. Nothing of importance.	
	5/9/17		Suffered by the line very heavy shelling of positions. Weather: Enemy sent to attack, repelling enemy. M.G. twice reported by infantry to be very effective. Two men wounded. My C.O. Sutton came up return to sections in the line. A.B.D. sections still in the line. A further two men it reported.	
	6/9/17		Remainder of company moves to "D" Lock camp BRANDHOEK. Ammunition ration carried up by C section.	
	7/9/17		Capt RANDS + Lt CATCHPOLE + Lt KIRKLAND went up the line to discover the situation of FROST Group up and section to relieve & sections on the line. Our teams carried out at MENIN GATE. Barrage fire laid on S.O.S. during the night 2000 rounds	

Army Form C. 2118.

WAR DIARY
or
INTELLIGENCE SUMMARY.
(Erase heading not required.)

448 th Fld Coy

Place	Date	Hour	Summary of Events and Information	Remarks and references to Appendices
BRANDHOEK	8/8/17		Day passed quietly. D.A.D.R. relieved. Damage guns fired on S.O.S. at dusk.	
	9/8/17		Everything comparatively quiet in the line. Sgt OSWIN relieved by 2/Lt EGGLETON. 2 O.R.'s wounded.	
H 16 d 6.2.	10/8/17		H.Q. moved from "Details Camp" to Transport Lines. # 16 A.S.B. Eight guns in the line relieved by 8 guns 225 Coy., the remaining four being in 126 E y RESERVE.	
	11/8/17		Lt FROST and his 2 guns arrive a/c being led astray by guide and relieve 2 guns in 126 E x RESERVE.	
	Mid.		Lt FROST goes down with trench feet, and the remaining four guns are relieved by 47 Coy. Five men killed at H16d by H.V. shell.	
	12/8/17		Lt EGGLETON goes down with gas. Company rests and cleans up.	

WAR DIARY or INTELLIGENCE SUMMARY

Army Form C. 2118.

148th M.G. Coy

Place	Date	Hour	Summary of Events and Information	Remarks and references to Appendices
H.bd.6.2.	14/9/17		Sent the Company under Lts ADAIR and CADWELL more up the line to relieve 8 guns of 275 M.G. Coy. Lts ADAIR and CADWELL reconnoitred positions for bringing guns in 2 days. Company HQ moves to RAMPARTS YPRES.	
Ramparts Ypres.	15/9/17		One officer from 47 bde & Ltg. Offs. C. Coy were attached to the Company, also 1 Officer + 20 ORs from 8th R.D.F. and 2 Lewis Gun teams with guns from HANTS (P). Capt CAMPBELL arrived. The rest of the company moved up to the line. 1/2 night.	
	10/9/17		The attack began zero hour 4.45 a.m. During the day six guns and one officer are put out of action. Towards evening guns are nearing on account of infantry withdrawal.	
	17/9/17		Day passed quietly and the company was relieved by 225 M.G. Coy. Return to ————	

Army Form C. 2118.

WAR DIARY
or
INTELLIGENCE SUMMARY.
(Erase heading not required.)

Lt E. P. M. G [?]

Place	Date	Hour	Summary of Events and Information	Remarks and references to Appendices
	7/8/17		Transport lines. No casualties on the way but HQ men took to transport lines tb.	
H 16 d	8/8/17		Company resting during the morning. Roll call taken 5th August. — 6 officers 34 OR. Total casualties — Sun kit sorted out, numbers pressed and entrained at VLAMERTINGHE to POPERINGHE when the Company marched to lands in WATOU "A" Area. Transport went on in front.	
WATOU "A" Area	10/8/17		Company rested, cleaned up generally — reported gun equipment. Only first guns were found to be missing. Worried by hostile aircraft all night.	
WORMHOUT	20/8/17		Moved off at 6am to billets in WORMHOUT. Company rested the remainder of the day.	
	21/8/17		Packing up again ready to entrain for the SOMME according to rumour. Marched to ESKELBECQ Station and entrained and left at 9.20 p.m.	

Army Form C. 2118.

WAR DIARY
or
INTELLIGENCE SUMMARY.
(Erase heading not required.)

48th M.G. Coy

Place	Date	Hour	Summary of Events and Information	Remarks and references to Appendices
COURCELLES	2/9/17		Arrived at BAPAUME (via ARRAS) about 7am and detrained. Proceeded to camp at COURCELLES preceded by the pipe band 2/9 NEA. Reported with large draft. Strength of company now 12 officers and 190 O.R.	
COURCELLES	3/9/17		Cleaning guns & equipment. The latter in preparation for inspection by G.O.C. Company inspected by G.O.C. & 8th Inf. Bde. 5.30 pm. Divisional Commander addresses all officers of Brigade on "The Division, Past, Present & Future".	
	4/9/17		Preparation for trenches anew. More preparation for trenches. Six new guns arrive. C.O. reconnoitres the line with D.M.G.O.	
	5/9/17		All guns tested. Company goes into the line, relieving 4 guns of 62 M.G. Coy and 12 of 237 M.G. Coy. H.Q. at TIPa 8.2 near CROISILLES. Attached men returned to Battalions	

WAR DIARY or INTELLIGENCE SUMMARY

Army Form C. 2118.

Place	Date	Hour	Summary of Events and Information	Remarks and references to Appendices
Field	27th Aug		Very quiet day in the line. No casualties. Very wet day and little work done.	
	28th Aug		Wrongful day. Beginning is getting material to improving R.E. dug-outs.	
	29th Aug		Quiet day. R.E. material now obtainable. Following gunmen relief on night 29/30th Aug 2 guns fired 1000 rounds on west side on roads through FONTAINE village at intervals during the night.	
	30th Aug		Lieut A.M. Adair and 4 N.C.O.s proceeded to CANIER'S for a course of Instruction at I.C. school. Coy improving their dug-outs and to advance to wood towards vilicers. The coy fired in 25 in through FONTAINE village.	

Army Form C. 2118.

WAR DIARY
INTELLIGENCE SUMMARY

(Erase heading not required.)

68th M.G. Coy.

Place	Date	Hour	Summary of Events and Information	Remarks and references to Appendices
Field	31st Aug		Lieutenant Fleming proceeded in the Company line attached infantry gun manner to rear batteries 1000 yds. behind the front in reserve and ammunition trench leading to DONING village	

D Campbell Capt
OC 68th M.G. Co

48 Coy. M.G.C.

SECRET

Reference Map Sheet 28 NW & NE /20000

48 Company M.G.C. less "C" Section will relieve 46th M.G.Coy with twelve guns on evening 3-8-17 in accordance with 16th Div[n] Instructions No E.S. 1287/1 d- 2-8-17, and will after relief come under orders of G.O.C. 47 Infantry Brigade

(2). The C.O. and Lts. ADAIR, OSWIN and CATCHPOLE will reconnoitre positions during early morning 3-8-17. leaving company H.Q at 3 A.M.

(3) DETAILS. "A" Section under 2nd Lt. C[   ]
B Section under Lt ADAIR and 2nd Lt [   ]
D Section under 2nd Lt OSWIN and 2nd Lt CATCHPOLE

4. B and D Sections guns and six belt boxes ammunition per gun, will be carried up to positions on pack animals.

A Sections guns as above will be carried on limbers to a point to be decided on during reconnaissance and from thence carried by hand.

5 (a) LT WALLACE will bring the company as detailed to the ASYLUM (H.12.D.) where they will be met by guides from 46 Company M.G.C. and officers doing reconnaissance

(b.) Guides will meet the company at ASYLUM (H.12.D) at 3. P.M.

6. Men will carry two days rations and emergency rations, one tin of water will be carried for each Sub-Section.

7. Position of S.A.A., water and ration dump will be notified later

Sheet 2.

Cont.

8. LT. WALLACE will remain at position of readiness (C.10.A & B) with rest of Company.

9. Relief will be completed by 7 P.M. 3-8-17. and reported to C.O. by runner by code issued to those concerned.

10. (a) Company H.Q. north of WILDE WOOD
    (b) 47 BDE. H.Q. at MILL COTT. (I.5.A.O.7.)

11. Please acknowledge.

E.W. Wallace LT.
O.C. Company MGC

Copies to:
1 and 2. War Diary.
3. C.O.
4. 2nd I/C.
5. T.O.
6, 7, 8, 9. O.C. A.B.C.D Sections
10. 48 BDE.
11. 47 BDE.
12. D.M.G.

48 Coy M.G.C.   Copy No 3.
W.D.

Secret.   Operation Orders
    Ref map sheet 28 NW & NE.   7-8-17

(1)(a) C section 48 Coy M.G.C. will relieve two gun
    teams of A Section, and two gun teams of D Section
    on the night of the 7th inst.
   (b) LT. E.H. FROST, with two gun teams of "C" Section
    will relieve 2ND LT. CALDWELL.
        LT. F.A. KIRKLAND, with two gun teams of "C"
    Section will relieve 2ND LT. P.A.H. OSWIN.

(2)(a) Rations will be carried up by ingoing teams
    from transport lines.
   (b) Relieving teams will be met by guides from
    sections concerned, at ADV. COY H.Q at WILDE
    WOOD at 6 P.M.
   (c) Relief to be complete by 7 P.M. Two guns and
    ammunition will be handed over by relieved teams.

(3) Two guides will accompany "C" section, and will
    bring relieved teams to Details Camp at G.12.D.2.4.
    They will await the relieved sections at HELL
    FIRE CORNER.
        Limbers taking "C" section's rations up, will
    wait with the guides at HELL FIRE CORNER, and
    will bring back personal equipment etc of the
    relieved teams

(4) LT. KIRKLAND will proceed in advance to make
    necessary arrangements for the relief.

Copies to
1 and 2 war diary   E. Wallace LT.
   3   C.O   48 COY. M.G.C.
   4,5 O.C "A" Section
   6,7   " B   "
   8,9   " C   "
   10,11 " D   "
   12   " T.O "
   13   " D.M.G.C.

SECRET.   No 48 Coy. M.G.C   Copy No. 1.

OPERATION ORDERS No. 39

Refce. Maps: FREZENBERG and Sheet 28 N.W.

In the Field.
9-8-1917.

1. On night of 10/11th August 1917 the following relief will take place.

2. Eight guns of this company will be relieved by 8 guns of the 225th Coy. M.G.C. in the following positions:-
   - 2 guns   FREZENBERG REDOUBT (D 25.c.8.5)
   - 2 guns.   NORTH STATION BUILDINGS (J 1 a. 5. 8)
   - 4 guns   IBEX RESERVE (I 6 central S to RAILWAY).

   The remaining 4 guns of this company will be withdrawn

3. On relief Company will move to Transport Lines at H.16.a.6.2.

4. The 225th Coy. M.G.C will take over all tripods and belt boxes at respective gun positions. The remainder of the belt boxes will be dumped at Company H.Q. Inventories to be taken and signed by incoming Section commanders.

5. All range cards in barrage lines to be handed over to relieving teams.

6. Four guides from Company H.Q will meet 8 gun teams of 225th Coy at ASYLEM, YPRES at 8 p.m. on 10th inst. These guides will conduct teams to ADVANCED COMPANY H.Q. (I 6. c 95.80) They will remain at Company HQ to guide relieved teams back to Transport Lines.

7. No teams will be withdrawn until they have been relieved by team of relieving formation. With the exception of the four gun teams being withdrawn.

8. LIEUT KIRKLAND will arrange to have guides from gun teams to be relieved at advanced Coy. HQ at 9 p.m on 10th inst.   (continued).

9. A limber will meet 4 gun teams to be withdrawn at ~~HELL FIRE CORNER~~ ASYLEM YPRES at 11 pm. LIEUT KIRKLAND will arrange what time these teams will leave the line.

10. LIEUT. BANNISTER will arrange about the above limber being sent. He will also arrange to have 2 limbers at ASYLEM, YPRES at 1 a.m. on 11th inst Section officers will arrange to place guns, and mens' kits in these limbers if necessary

11. Completion of relief to be reported to D.M.G.O. 16th DIVISION by O.C. this Company.

12. Acknowledge.

E. W. Wallace LT.
No. 48 Coy. M.G.C.

Issued at 7.....a.m.
Copies to :

1 & 2	War Diary	9	D.M.G.O. 16th Division
3	C.O.	10	G.O.C. 48th Inf. Bde.
4	Transport Officer	11	O.C. 225 Coy. M.G.C.
5	O.C. "A" Section	12	
6	" "B" "	13	
7	" "C" "	14	
8	" "D" "		

Secret.   Copy 1

No. 98 Coy. M.G.C.
Preliminary Instructions & Information for Machine Guns.

1. Offensive operations, in which Machine Guns of this Brigade will co-operate, will shortly take place.

2. (a) Zero hour and date will be notified later.
   (b) Objective – to capture and consolidate enemy's trenches up to, and including dotted RED line.
   (c) The infantry will halt for 20 minutes on the GREEN line.

3. (a) Twelve guns of this company will be allotted for barrage fire. These guns will be divided into batteries of 4 guns each.
   (b) Approximate positions :-
        RIGHT BATTERY .... D. b. 86. 85
        CENTRE BATTERY .... D20. a. 45. 15.
        LEFT BATTERY .... D20. c. 4. 5.
   (c) CENTRE BATTERY – 4 guns of "B" Section under LIEUT ADAIR.
       LEFT BATTERY – 2 guns of "D" Section and 2 guns of "A" Section
                                               under LIEUT EDWARDS.
       RIGHT BATTERY – 2 guns of "C" Section and 2 guns of "D" Section
                                               under Lt. KIRKLAND & 2Lt. OSWIN

4. The lifts and times will not be departed from as long as the attack proceeds as planned. To be notified later.
   In the event of any portion of the line being held up the machine guns will come under the orders of the G.O.C.

5. (a) The barrage will be worked on a time table to be notified later.
   (b) 80,000 rounds per battery, together with oil and water will be dumped at approximate battery positions before ZERO day.

6. (a) At ZERO plus, (to be notified later) when barrage guns cease firing, 2 guns of "D" Section under 2 Lieut Oswin will proceed to a position near POTSDAM (D 26. c). Barrage lines for these 2 guns to be notified later.
   (b) They will arrange to draw S.A.A. from original barrage positions.

7. (a) Two guns per battalion for consolidation will go forward from the assembly points in rear of two attacking battalions.
   (b) Two guns of "C" Section under Lieut FROST, in rear of right attacking battalion will move to position on Roadway about D 26. b. 50. 45.
                                                (Continued)

(Para. 7 continued)
Two guns of "A" Section under 2Lieut CALDWELL, in rear of Left attacking battalion will move forward to suitable position about BREMEN REDOUBT.

(c) These four guns will not be used for barrage or indirect fire until they are sufficiently supplied with S.A.A. In case of necessity Battalion Commanders can divert these guns to other positions for purpose of defence.

INFORMATION

8. BRIGADE BATTLE H.Q. will be at ST JEAN FARM. ADVANCED BRIGADE FORWARD REPORTING CENTRE will be at FREZENBERG REDOUBT and thence after capture of dotted RED line to VAMPIR FARM.

9. After capture of RED dotted line RIGHT and LEFT assaulting battalion H.Qs will move to POTSDAM and VAMPIR FARM respectively.

10. The magnetic bearing of the advance is 75°.
Further details will be issued later.

In the Field.   E. W. Ballard, Lt.
11-8-1917   No. 48 Coy. M.G.C.

Copies to:
1 & 2 War Diary   8   O.C. 2 R.D.F
3   O.C.   9   9th R.D.F.
4   Transport Officer   10 8th R.D.F.
5   D.M.G.O. 16th Div.   11 File.
6   G.O.C. 48th Inf. Bde. 12 & 13 Section Officers.
7   O.C. 7th R.I.R.

SECRET.

48th MACHINE GUN COMPANY.

OPERATION ORDER. NO. 40.

Employment of Machine Guns in the Advance from the
BLACK Line.

Reference Map - FREZENBERG 1/10,000.

1. The 16 guns of this Company will be employed in the forth-coming Operations as follows:-

    4 guns will be attached to the attacking Battalions.
    12 guns under the D.M.G.O. for barrage fire.

2. **BARRAGE.**

    (a) The 12 barrage guns, under Lieut. F.A. KIRKLAND, will be divided into 3 batteries of 4 guns each, with one officer in command of each battery:-

    Left battery (marked "H" on map) - 2/Lt. OSWIN.
    Centre battery (marked "J" on map) - Lt. ADAIR.
    Right battery (marked "K" on map) - 2/Lt. CALDWELL.

    (b) The approximate positions of these 3 batteries at ZERO are shown on Appendix A1.

    (c) The barrage will work according to a time-table shown on Appendix B. The calculations must be checked by battery commanders. The figures given are based on the assumption that the guns are in the exact positions shown on the map. If these positions are not actually occupied, battery commanders must make necessary alterations and report positions to C.O. immediately.

    (d) The various barrage zones are shown on attached map.

    (e) In the event of the attacking Battalions of this Brigade being held up these 12 guns will come under the orders of G.O.C., 48th. Brigade.

3. On capture of dotted RED Line, 2 guns of 47th. Machine Gun Company will move from their barrage positions to positions about POTSDAM (D 28 c).
    The two guns will lay on Protected Barrage Line No. 4. They will arrange to draw S.A.A. from original barrage positions.

4. **CONSOLIDATION.**

    (a) The 4 guns which have been placed at the disposal of the two attacking Battalions for consolidation, will ~~go for-ward with~~ *follow* the Battalions to which they have been allotted, and take up the approximate positions as shown on Appendix A2.

    (b) They will not be used for barrage or indirect fire until sufficiently supplied with S.A.A., when they will lay on G.O.C. Barrage Line No. 4, as shown on attached map.

48th. M.G. Coy. O.O. No. 10.   Page 2.

(c) In case of necessity Commanders of battalions to which these guns have been allotted can divert them to other positions for purpose of defence.

5. **AMMUNITION.**

Main S.A.A. Dump at MILL COT.
Advanced S.A.A. Dump at D 25 c 5.0.
Dumps will also be formed at battery positions before ZERO hour.

6. **COMMUNICATIONS.**

(a) Advanced Brigade Forward Report Centre will be at FREZEN-BERG REDOUBT.

(b) Advanced Company Forward Report Centre will be at IRON RESERVE (I 6 c 85.75).

(c) Company Headquarters will be at RAMPARTS, YPRES (attached 48th Infantry Brigade H.Q.)

(d) Headquarters of Battalions at ZERO:-

    7th. Rl. Irish Rifles — D 25 d 3.4. (Right Battn.)
    9th~~2nd~~ Rl. Dublin Fusrs — D 25 d 5.0. (Left Battn.)
    ~~2nd " " "~~ — FREZENBERG REDOUBT.

7. **GENERAL.**

(a) Full use must be made of pack mules for supplying guns with S.A.A. and water. Lieut. BANISTER will make all necessary arrangements and will have 20 attached men at his disposal. Rations and water will be sent to IRON RESERVE (I 6 c 85.75).

(b) All available belts and belt boxes are to be taken up to gun positions on Y/Z night.

(c) Every man will carry at least two bandoliers of S.A.A. Those men not carrying gun material will carry four bandoliers.

(d) Map referred to is G/10/B, map to accompany 16th Division G.S. Instruction No. 14.

8. **ACKNOWLEDGE.**

Issued at   2 p.m.

                    F A Kirkland.
14.8.1917.   Lieutenant,
                    48th Machine Gun Company.

APPENDIX A.

Reference of 1:1000 map:

Battery	O.C. Battery	Composition of Battery	Approximate Position of Battery
Left (H)	Lt. F.A.H. Dawin	3 teams "D" Sections plus. 1 team "C" Section	D 25. c. 50. 85.
Centre (J)	Lt. A.M. Adair	3 teams "D" Section plus 1 team "C" Section	D 25. c. 99. 18.
Right (K)	2nd Lt. J. Caldwell	3 teams "A" Section plus 1 team "C" Section	J. 1. b. 20. 90.

APPENDIX A 2

Battalion	O.C. Sub-Section	Composition of Sub-Section	Approximate Position to be taken up.
7th R.I.R.	2nd Lt. Webb.	1 team "A" Section 1 team "B" Section	Roadway about D 26. b 80. 45. TO FIRE S.E.
9th R.D.F.	2nd Lt. Jamson	1 team "C" Section 1 team "D" Section	GREMIN REDOUBT. TO FIRE N.E.

APPENDIX B

Barrage	Time Table	Battery	Q.E.	Direction	Traverse	Rate of Fire	Remarks
1.	ZERO to ZERO plus 8	Left	2°0'	51°	2°	250 per 2 min	
		Centre	2°0'	60°	2°	250 per 2 min	
		Right	2°0'	53°	1°	250 per 2 min	
2.	ZERO plus 8 to ZERO plus 30	Left	3°57'	56°	2°	Intense	
		Centre	2°46'	62°	2°	Intense	
		Right	2°46'	57°	2°	Intense	
3. & S.O.S.	ZERO plus 30 to ZERO plus 120	Left	8°23'	60°	2°	250 per 5 min	From ZERO +120 to ZERO +150 fire at the rate of one belt per 15 minutes.
		Centre	7°27'	66°	2°	250 per 5 min	
		Right	7°27'	63°	2°	250 per 5 min	
4.							

(Direction: GRID BEARING)

SECRET.

40th MACHINE GUN COMPANY.

OPERATION ORDERS NO. 41.

1. On the night 14-15 August the following relief will take place.

2. 8 guns of 205th Machine Gun Company, at present in the line, will be relieved by 8 guns of this Company.

3. Lieut. ADAMS, with one section (4 guns), and 2nd. Lieut. CALDWELL, with one section (4 guns), will be at ESSEX FARM SIDING at 11.30 p.m., to meet guides of gun teams to be relieved.

4. All tripods and belt boxes at respective gun positions will be taken over. Inventories to be taken and signed.

5. Range cards and barrage lines to be taken over by relieving teams.

6. Completion of relief to be reported to the C.O.

7. On the night 14th-15th, 40th. Company H.Q. will move to the RAMPARTS, YPRES (48th Infantry Brigade H.Q).

8. ACKNOWLEDGE.

Issued at 11 A M

E. Wallace
Lieutenant,
40th Machine Gun Company.

14.8.1917.

Copies to:-

1. C.O.
2. 2nd I/C.
3. & 4. Section Officers.
5. O.C., 205th. M.G. Coy.
6. O.O.C.
7. FILE. ✓
8.

SECRET. Copy No 9.

48th. INFANTRY BRIGADE

ORDER NO. 149.

17th August 1917.

Reference Sheets - 27 and 28. 1/40,000.

1. The Brigade will move from Camp in VLAMERTINGHE No. 3. Area to WATOU No "A" Area on 18th instant.

2. Units (less Transport) will entrain at VLAMERTINGHE in accordance with Time-Table as under:-

	Parade at Station at:-
(a) 7th Rl. Irish Rifles.	2. 20. P.M.
9th Rl. Dublin Fusiliers.	2. 25. "
48th Brigade Headquarters.	2. 30. "
2nd Rl. Dublin Fusiliers.	3. 40. P.M.
8th Rl. Dublin Fusiliers.	3. 45. "
(48th M.G.Company.	4. 0. "
(155th Field Company, R.E.	4. 0. "

(b) Adjutants will meet Brigade Major at Station as under:-

Adjutants of 7th Rl.Irish Rifles and 9th Rl. Dublin Fusiliers, at 2. 0. P.M.
Adjutants of remaining Units at 3. 30. P.M.

3. Units will detrain under Battalion arrangements on arrival at POPERINGHE and march to same camps previously occupied by them in WATOU, No. "A" Area.

4. All Transport will move by road under orders of Brigade Transport Officer subject to following restrictions:-

(a) Transport may not enter POPERINGHE before 4. 0. P.M.

(b) Main Road EAST of POPERINGHE is not to be used.

(c) WEST of POPERINGHE route will be road in L 9.a. and B.

5. Transport of Units will use same camps as previously occupied at WATOU.

6. 145th Company, A.S.C., will march independently.

ACKNOWLEDGE.

ISSUED AT 10. 0 P.M.

Captain,
Brigade Major, 48th Infantry Brigade.

Copies to:-
1 & 2 War Diary.
3. G.O.C.
4. Filo.
5. 7th Irish Rifles.
6. 2nd. Dublins.
7. 8th. Dublins.
8. 9th. Dublins.
9. 48th M.G.Company.
10. Staff Captain, 48th Bde.
11. 16th Division "Q"
12. 16th Division "G"
13. 145th Coy., A.S.C.
14. 47th Inf. Brigade.
15. 49th Inf. Brigade.
16. 48th Bde. T.O.
17. 155th Fld. Coy. R.E.
18.

O.C. 47th M.G.Coy.
     48th M.G.Coy.
     49th M.G.Coy.

16th Div.No. D.M.G.O. 100/1.   17th AUGUST 1917.

    I have sent your O.C. in the line a copy of the attached orders.

    Please arrange with him when and where he wants his limbers in YPRES to-night, to bring guns, etc.

    Every available man in your lines should be sent up to help out with the relief.   Nothing must be left behind.   Enough has, I fear, been lost already.

    I reply on Os.C. to do everything they can to get all their material out of the line.

                                      Major. D.M.G.O.
                                      16th Division.

S E C R E T.

    47th M.G.Coy.
    48th M.G.Coy.
    49th M.G.Coy.
    47th Inf.Bde.
    48th Inf.Bde.
    49th Inf.Bde.
    46th Inf.Bde.
   225th M.G.Coy.
    46th M.G.Coy.

16th Div. No. D.M.G.O. 100/3. 17th AUGUST 1917.

---

1. On the night August 17/18th the following reliefs will take place.

2. 12 guns of the 49th M.G.Coy. will be relieved by 12 Guns of the 46th M.G.Coy. at :-

    SQUARE FARM. 8 Guns.
    FREZENBERG X ROADS (D.25.c.25.90). 4 Guns.

3. 12 Guns of the 48th M.G.Coy. will be relieved by 12 Guns of the 225th M.G.Coy. at :-

    About J.1.a.8.8. 4 Guns.
    BILL COTTAGE. 2 Guns.
    IBEX RESERVE. 6 Guns.

The last 2 positions not now being occupied by 48th M.G.Coy. 225th M.G.Coy. will occupy these positions, and when occupied O.C. 48th M.G.Coy. can withdraw an equivalent number of guns (8) from his barrage position.

4. When reliefs, as provided for above, are complete Os.C. 48th and 49th M.G.Coys. will withdraw all surplus guns.

5. 47th M.G.Coy. will withdraw all guns in position at midnight August 17th/18th.

6. On relief 47th, 48th and 49th M.G.Coys. will proceed to their respective transport lines in the VLAMERTINGHE area H.16.d.

7. 49th M.G.Coy. will hand over to 46th M.G.Coy. 12 Tripods, also 8 belt boxes per gun.

8. 48th M.G.Coy. will hand over to 225th M.G.Coy. 4 Tripods.

9. An equivalent number of Tripods will be collected from the 46th and 225th M.G.Coys. from their transport lines.

10. Remaining Tripods and belt boxes will be withdrawn from the line on relief.

11. Guides for Guns at FREZENBERG X ROADS and J.1.a.8.8. will be provided by 49th and 48th M.G.Coys. respectively. They will meet the relieving teams at MENIN GATE at 8.15 p.m., August 17th.

12. All range cards and barrage lines to be handed over to relieving teams.

13. ACKNOWLEDGE.

R. Le Butt
Major. D.M.G.O.
16th Division.

S E C R E T   Copy No. 59

16TH. DIVISION ADMINISTRATIVE ORDER NO. 31.

REFERENCE 16TH. DIVISION
ORDER NO. 152..........

19th. August 1917.

1.   The Division will entrain in accordance with the attached tables.

    The times of arrivals are approximate only. Detraining Stations will be notified later.

2.   G.O's.C.Brigades are responsible for the entraining arrangements at Stations as under :-

    CAESTRE .... G.O.C., 47th. Inf. Bde.
    CASSELL .... G.O.C., 49th. Inf. Bde.
    ESQUELBECQ ...... G.O.C., 48th. Inf. Bde.

3.   Arrangements should be made by Brigades concerned to control traffic on the road approaches to the entraining stations, and no troops or transport should be allowed to enter the Station Yards until the R.T.O. is ready.

5. (a) All trains consist of 1 Officers carriage: 17 flat
4.   trucks: 30 covered trucks.
    (b) (i) Each flat truck will take an average of 4 axles.
        (ii)Each covered truck will take 6 H.D. Horses,
                      or 8 L.D. Horses or mules,
                      or 40 men.
    (c) No personnel or stores will be allowed in the brake vans at each end of the train, or on the roofs of the trucks.
    No covered trucks should be used for baggage as it restricts space available for personnel.

5.   A fatigue party of 2 Officers and 100 men will de detailed for duty at each of the entraining and detraining stations. Those for the detraining Stations will travel on the first train of the move and those for the entraining Stations on the last train.

6.   An Officer answering for the Brigade will remain at the entraining Station until the last train of his Brigade Group is ready to be despatched.

7.   Transport of Inf. Battalions will arrive at the Station three hours, and the personnel 1½ hours, before the departure of the train.

    Other Units will arrive three hours before the departure of the trains.

8.   A complete marching out state, shewing the numbers of men, horses, G.S., Limbered G.S., and 2 wheeled wagons and bicycles, should be sent down with the transport of every Unit, so that accommodation in the train can be checked by the R.T.O. at the beginning of the entrainment.

P.T.O. for para. 9.

9. Supply and baggage wagons will accompany their own units in every case.

10. The entrainment of all units must be completed half an hour before the time of departure of train.

11. Breast ropes for horse trucks must be provided by the Units themselves: ropes for lashing vehicles on the flat trucks will be provided by the Railway.

12. Pickets must be provided at all stops for each end of the train to prevent troops leaving.

13. All doors of covered trucks and carriages on the right-hand side of the train, when on the main line, should be kept closed.

14. The Senior Officer present will be responsible for the entraining and detraining of all troops in his train.

15. The Divl. Supply Column and Motor Ambulance vehicles will proceed by road on 21st. and 22nd. instant, in such detachments as may be necessary, and will report to S.M.T.O., BEHAGNIES on arrival.

16. Supply arrangements will be as follows :-

"A" for troops entraining on 21st. instant.
"B" for troops entraining on 22nd. instant.

"A" (1) S.S.O. has drawn P.M. from Railhead today, for consumption on 21st. - (Day of entrainment.)

(2) Rations for consumption 22nd. will be drawn from Railhead on 20th. by Div. Train.
The Supply Wagons containing these supplies will entrain full with their Units on 21st.

(3) Rations for consumption on 23rd. will be drawn by No. 4 D.S.C. from WIPPENHOEK on 21st. This portion of the Supply Column will proceed full to new Area.

"B" (1) S.S.O. will draw P.M. from Railhead on 20th. for consumption on 22nd. - (Day of Entrainment.)

(2) Rations for consumption 23rd. will be drawn by the D.S.C. from Railhead, WIPPENHOEK on 21st.
Div. Train will load these rations at Refilling Point, and the Supply Wagons will entrain full with their own Units.

Supply Officers of 47th. and 49th. Inf. Bdes. with their supply details will proceed by the first train of the respective Brigade Groups.

Supply Officer of 48th. Inf. Bde. Group will proceed by last train of 48th. Inf. Bde. Group. This Officer will superintended the rationing of all Units while in this Area, who are out of touch with their own Supply Officers.

"A" & "Q",　　　　　　　　　　　　　　　　　　　　Lieut-Colonel,
16th. Division.　　　　　　　　　　　　　A.A. & Q.M.G., 16th. Division.
　　　For distribution see over.

SECRET.   Copy No. 10.

48th Infantry Brigade

ORDER NO. 181.

20th August 1917.

Map Reference Sheet LENS No. 11. 1/100,000 (2nd Edition)
              Sheet   27. 1/40,000.

1.   The 48th Infantry Brigade Group will move by train on the 21st and 22nd August to join the Third Army.

2.   Entraining Station will be ESQUELBECQ.
      Detraining Station will be BAPAUME HALT.

3.   Entrainment and Detrainment will be carried out in accordance with 16th Division Administrative Order No 31 attached.

4.   (a) 10th Rl. Dublin Fusiliers will detail 2 Officers and 100 Other Ranks for duty at Entraining Station, party to report in the first instance to 2/Lieut. HAMMOND, 2nd Rl. Dublin Fusiliers, at Station at 10 a.m. on 21st instant.
      This party may be relieved on departure of any train by a similar party under Battalion arrangements

      (b) This party will travel by last train which leaves at 5.20 P.M. on 22nd August.

5.   On arrival of first train at detraining Station a detraining party of 2 Officers and 100 Other ranks will be furnished as under:-
                7th Rl. Irish Rifles............1 Officer. 50. O.R.
                10th Rl. Dublin Fusiliers......1 Officer. 50. O.R.
      to report to detraining Officer, Lieut. SETH-SMITH, 7th. Rl. Irish Rifles.

6.   This party will be relieved by 1 Officer and 50 O.R. from 2nd Rl. Dublin Fusiliers and 1 Officer and 50 O.R. from a Company of 10th Rl. Dublin Fusiliers travelling with 2nd. Rl. Dublin Fusiliers to report for duty to detraining Officer at Station at 12 noon on 22nd instant.

7.   Units will detail Billeting Parties to travel by train leaving at 1.20 P.M. on 21st instant as under:-
            1 Officer and 4 O.R. per Battalion.
            1 Officer and 1 O.R. for each other Unit.
            Bicycles should be brought and rations for consumption on 21st and 22nd inst.

8.   ACKNOWLEDGE.

ISSUED AT 7.15. P.M.
                                         T B Brady
                                                Captain,
                                Brigade Major, 48th Infantry Brigade.

Copies to:-
1 & 2 War Diary.	10. 48th M.G.Coy.	18. 48th Bde.T.O.
3. File.	11. 48th T.M.Bty.	19. 155th Fd.Coy.Rl
4. G.O.C.	12. Staff Captain.	20. 112th F.Amb.
5. 7th Irish Rif.	13. 16th Divn. "Q"	21. ADMS, 16th Div.
6. 2nd. Dublins.	14. 16th Divn. "G"	22. Bde Signals.
7. 8th. Dublins.	15. 145th Coy.ASC.	23. R.T.O.
8. 9th. Dublins.	16. 47th Inf.Bde.	ESQUELBECQ.
9. 10th. Dublins.	17. 49th Inf.Bde.	24.
	25.	
	26.	

No 48 Coy. M.G.C

Operation Orders

21-8-17

(1) The Company will entrain tonight at ESQUELBECQ Station at 9-20 P.M.
Transport must be at Station 3 hours before time of departure of train.
Separate Orders will be issued by Transport Officer as to time of leaving Camp

(2) The Company will parade at Company Head-Quarters at 6-15 and will march off at 6-30 p.m

(3) Dress :- Full Marching Order

(4) All Officer's Valises and remaining Q.M. Stores must be packed on limbers by 4-30 p.m

(5) Rations for tomorrow will be distributed to day to sections

E. W. Wallace LIEUT
No 48 Coy. M.G.C

Copies to :-
1 & 2 War Diaries
3 C.O
4 2⁰ I/C
5 Officers Mess
6. Transport Officer
7. File
8.
9.
10.

Copy of Report
24/11/17

To. D.M.G.O.   16th Division.

Report on the action of M.G's 20/11/17

The 48th M.G. Co. cooperated in the attack by the 16th Division on TUNNEL TR. and TUNNEL SUPPORT by firing a barrage according to the scheme laid down in "16th Div. Instructions for an Offensive Action, Instruction No. 3."

The barrage positions taken up by the Company were:-

    No. 6 Group.   CRUX ROAD (u.19.c)
    No. 7 Group.   BULL ROAD (u.19.D.)

The constitution of these groups are as follows:-

No. 6 Group. { "C" Section 48th M.G. Co. Lieut.
             { "D" Section 48th M.G. Co. F.A. Kirkland
             { 1 Section 49th M.G. Co. i/c Group.

No. 7 Group. { A. Section 48th M.G. Co. Lieut
             { B. Section 48th M.G. Co. A. McAdam
             { 1 Section 49th M.G. Co. i/c Group

H.Q. of the former Group were Crux Road (u.19.c.
   " " " latter Group were Bull Road u.19.D.
   " " " Company   " FACTORY. CROISILLES

By 4 p.m. 19/11/17. all guns of both Groups were in position and guns laid on their Barrage lines.

During the night 19th/20th 6 guns of No. 6 Group kept up intermittent fire on the enemy tracks and C.T's and displayed the usual normal activity. The following targets were engaged:- Tracks in V.15.D.
                                        SUNKEN ROAD V.15.C.
                                        FAG ALLEY.
                                        OLDENBURGH LANE.

2.

No. 7 Group lay quiet all night.

Action of No. 6 Group after Zero hour.

6-20 A.M. to 7.50 A.M.	At Zero hour 6-20 a.m. all guns opened rapid fire on their barrage lines, the times being taken from the artillery behind, which fired a salvo at Zero hour as a signal for all guns to open fire together. After 20 minutes one gun was put out of action, owing to a defect in Mechanism. No shells fell nearer than RAILWAY RESERVE. 85,000 rounds were fired.
8.30 A.M. to 9.25 a.m.	Having fixed the allotted barrage. Guns were cleaned and barrels changed. 4 guns then fired on secondary targets. FAG ALLEY and MATCH ALLEY — 3000 rounds were fired.
9.25 a.m. to 9.55 a.m.	On message being received from D.M.G.O. a concentration was ordered on the Sunken road in V.15.A. where enemy was reported massing for Counter attack. Fire was maintained till 9.55 a.m. 4000 rounds were fired.
9.55 a.m. to 4.30 pm	Secondary targets were again engaged and intermittent fire kept up. 40,000 rounds were fired.
4.50 pm to 5.30 pm	Following intense M.G. Fire on the left group opened a slow rate of fire on S.O.S lines. Fire then ceased on S.O.S lines and secondary targets were again engaged. 7000 rounds were fired in good lines as per above.
3.0 pm to 10. p.m.	30,000 rounds were fired on Secondary targets.

3.

10 p.m. to 11.10 p.m.	Fire was suspended owing to our patrol being out during those hours.
	After 11-10 p.m. guns returned to Normal S.O.S. and secondary targets and intermittent fire kept up all through the night.
	50.000 rounds were fired during this period.
	The damaged gun was replaced on the night 20th/21st.
6.40 a.m. to 7.10 a.m. to 8.0 a.m.	At 6.40 a.m. the S.O.S. signal was sent up by our troops and all guns at once opened rapid fire and kept up this rate of fire for 30 minutes, then a slow rate of fire was kept up until the situation became Normal again.
	The guns were put out of action owing to mechanical defects.
	After 8 a.m. 21st inst, the situation became again Normal.

Action of No. 7 Group after Zero hour.

6.20 a.m. to 7.50 a.m.	At Zero hour 6.20 a.m. all guns opened rapid fire on their barrage lines. Enemy retaliated fairly heavily on this Group, and after half an hour, several casualties were caused. These were confined to the 49th M.G. Section attached.
	90.000 rounds were fired during this period.
	Guns were then cleaned and barrels changed and guns laid on S.O.S. lines
	Guns then engaged the secondary targets laid down for them.

4.

9.25 A.M. to 10. A.M.	On message received from D.M.G.O. target Sunken road in U.8.a. was engaged. Guns were got on this target very quickly, this being largely due to the action of Lieut A. M. Adair. 8 Guns concentrated on this road while the remaining four traversed. 30.000 rounds were fired.
10.a.m. to 4.50 p.m.	Intermittent fire was then kept up on the allotted positions. 50.000 rounds were fired. At 4.50 p.m. Guns took up the S.O.S. rate of fire owing to intense M.G. fire on left. 5.000 rounds were fired.
4.50 pm to 10 p.m.	After the situation returned to the Normal, Guns fired on Secondary target till 10 p.m. 30.000 rounds were fired.
10 p.m. to 11-10.p.m.	Guns laid on a different barrage, between these hours, while Infantry patrols were out. After 11.10 p.m. Guns again returned to firing on the Secondary targets. 40,000 rounds fired during night.
11-10 pm to 6.40 a.m.	At 6.40 a.m. on the 21st inst S.O.S. was sent up by our own troops, and all guns opened "rapid" The enemy shelling on these positions was very heavy indeed, and during this period, I regret to state that Lieut A. M. Adair Officer i/c Group was instantaneously killed by a shell. I take this opportunity of paying tribute to the excellent work done by this gallant officer during the operations under consideration.

WAR DIARY.

FOR MONTH OF SEPTEMBER, 1917.

VOLUME 18

UNIT:— M.G.C. 8th Machine Gun Coy

WAR DIARY
or
INTELLIGENCE SUMMARY.

(Erase heading not required.)

Army Form C. 2118.

SECRET

Place	Date	Hour	Summary of Events and Information	Remarks and references to Appendices
CROISILLES	1st Sept.		Coys of M.G. Coy from Guards Div. Buried dead	
			W 45th Coy came in T.17.d.6.2.	
			Guns S.3. withdrawn to right flank	
			of night from M.E.B.4. Guns taken	
			from coys to 4 Posn. L.N.3. standards	
			2 recorded slight hostile shelling	
			of Station Area track & Noreuil Road	
	2nd Sept.		2 officers & 19 O.R. holding ammunition Pt. 17. to W. of SWITCH	
			at Cow. occupied 2 positions in LY sector	
			in the vicinity of SH. PT. TRENCH	
	3rd Sept.		4 guns of 45th Coy to relieve 2 Div. about Junction	
			back to advance post to R.W. Railway EMBANKMENT	
			20th D Coy LEGER	
			R.W.D. taking to work reconnoitred new position	
			6 A. R. in night chol	
	4th Sept.		2nd Lieut TILLN relieved from leave	
			Trench Comm. quiet except for one night on by special	
	5th Sept.		Situation had unchanged	

WAR DIARY or INTELLIGENCE SUMMARY

Army Form C. 2118.

Place	Date	Hour	Summary of Events and Information	Remarks and references to Appendices
CROISILLES	6th		CAPT D CAMPBELL proceeds on leave to MELUN. About 6 heavy shells fell in vicinity of Guards Div camp. R.E's returned to H.Q Aug 6th. Transport working on supplies at ERVILLERS.	
do	7th		R.F.A Shells again fell in our C.P.Q. Afternoon very quiet. 2 sections relieved "C" Section in left sector	
do	8th		Very quiet all day. R.E's trench work at M.D Dugins shewed fire at night. Heavy M.G's trying above at night	
do	9th		Very quiet day. The Div HQ a QUARRY EAST OF ECOIVRES. Conference of O's C Coys on B/1294. Dr. G.O. present.	
do	10th		"C" section relieved "B" section at 11.4.5 S.S	
do	11th		DR G.O. R.E's work guns. Usual work and repair firing. 2 guns at F 2.3 relieved by 4.6 relief Two teams	
do	12th		proceed to new posture at JUNCTION of RIVER RD and M.M.D TR. Bridge main guns.	
do	13th		Work started at ERVILLERS for new Camp. The guys	

WAR DIARY
INTELLIGENCE SUMMARY

Army Form C. 2118.

18th Coy M.G.C.

Place	Date	Hour	Summary of Events and Information	Remarks and references to Appendices
CROISELLES	13th Sept	Cont	Weather changed to the worse. Work on H.Q. Regt. and Batt. nearing completion.	
do	14th Sept		Making preparations for operations of 15th to take place on R. 38th Divisions on left and 52nd Division on right.	
do	15th Sept		S.O.S. (B & D) [Vickers] Cooperate with operations on left. Zero hour 3pm. 4:30pm r. 7.40 pm. 3, 60,000 rds fired. "RED FLAG" ahead. No damage. Very little retaliation.	
do	16th Sept		All quiet again after 3" shell of operations at 4:30 pm. Never work by day, not by night. Hostile aircraft active but [illegible] flying away high.	
do	17th Sept		"B" Section relieve "C" Section 49th with to take over position at H.Q1. New Defence scheme issued and all M.G. positions renumbered. 18th Regt and Junction Work on concrete emplacement at CROISELLES taken hand by the R.E's.	
do	18th Sept		Our Coys moved from RIVER ROAD to 47A. Reserve Line	

Army Form C. 2118.

WAR DIARY
or
INTELLIGENCE SUMMARY.
(Erase heading not required.)

6th Coy M.E.C.

Place	Date	Hour	Summary of Events and Information	Remarks and references to Appendices
CROISELLES	18th Sept	G.18	Moved from RAILWAY EMBANKMENT & ST LEGER & ECOUVILLERS	
do	19th Sept		CROISELLES very heavily shelled all day. Very annoying	
			where H.T.M. bombardment & guns gunpits. Good 25 front	
do	20th Sept		"A" section relieves "D" section in SHAFT TRENCH	
do	21st Sept		Capt R. CAMPBELL returns from leave. Hard work on	
			emplacements. A Aug-not Sinclair & St Aug-not Trench	
			by team at Coy HQ.	
do	22nd Sept		Bombed "A" Coy 20 mm guns near heights	
			found chief trouble being CROISELLES- HENDECOURT	
			road and FONTAINE - HENDECOURT road	
do	23rd Sept		Very quiet day. No firing was done on anyone	
			owing to Infantry Patrols being out	
do	24th Sept		O.C. Coy visits guns in left sector. Good progress when	
do	25th Sept		"D" section relieves "C" section in position 43 & 44P,	
			45A & 46A. A new AA position being built	
			at Coy HQ. 2nd Lieut WILSON relieving 2nd Lt. BLUNDELL	

WAR DIARY
INTELLIGENCE SUMMARY.

48th Coy. M.G.C.

Place	Date	Hour	Summary of Events and Information	Remarks and references to Appendices
OOSTHOEK	26th Sept		New RANGE CHARTS being made up for Coy on line. Training Cloth. Trench Standing Order issued by D.M.G.O. and one man in each position.	
do	27th Sept		Limbers working as a coy. M. Coy 3rd in incement grenades to the Brigade Bomb Store. No 2 in carry party returned to Coy HQ for the purpose of making more material. H.T in bombardment in afternoon. M.G's Cooperate	
do			Aug. arcs. H.T in bombardment on PRINCE TRENCH and 6000 rounds on Zones on CEYLON TRENCH. Guns 6000 rounds an fixed in CEYLON TRENCH. (PUG AV.) firing 42.A.Y.3.A.J. also 48.I.V.11. (PUG AV.)	
do	28th Sept		Gas Barrage on FUN LANE which was turn on in previous night. Tung made.	
do	29th Sept		United Gunns in left sector All Crept and Good progress being made Reconnoissance for a new position to incremebt J 4.7 a. Coy SUPPORT also reconnoitred and found consistahr for a M.G. influence	

Army Form C. 2118.

WAR DIARY
or
INTELLIGENCE SUMMARY

(Erase heading not required.)

48th Coy M.G.C.

Place	Date	Hour	Summary of Events and Information	Remarks and references to Appendices
CROISILLES	30th Sept.		Very quiet day. Maps - making and working out calculations for guns. Each gun position now in possession of "TRENCH STANDING ORDERS" + "RANGE CHART." New A.A. position near 46.11 now completed.	

Dampier Capt. M.G.C.
Comdg. 48th Coy M.G.C.

S E C R E T.

47th M.G.Coy.
48th M.G.Coy.
49th M.G.Coy.

47th Inf.Bde.)
48th Inf.Bde.)
49th Inf.Bde.)   for information.
50th Division.)

16th Div.No. D.M.G.O.140.   11th SEPTEMBER 1917.

1. The Machine Guns of the 16th Division will co-operate in a minor operation, about which further details will be issued, against the enemy trenches WEST of CHERISY on Zero day. *with the 50th Div.*

2. Reference attached Map - 16 Machine Guns of the 16th Division will be allotted tasks as follows:-

        47th M.G.Coy.   4 guns.
        48th M.G.Coy.   8 guns.
        49th M.G.Coy.   4 guns.

in 2 Groups:-

        E   8 guns.
        E 1   8 guns.

3. All Officers M.G.Coys. will reconnoitre these positions, and work out the necessary calculations, so as to have everything ready by 13th September 1917. All guns to be in position by 12 Noon on Zero day.

4. Officers of the M.G.Coys. will check watches with A. Group 151 M.G.Coy. at FARMERS LANE at 2 p.m. on Zero Day.

5. The programme of firing will be as follows:-

FIRST PHASE.	Rate of Fire.
Zero. All groups open fire.	Zero to Zero plus 5 min. 1 belt per min. Zero plus 5 min. to Zero plus 20 min. 1 belt per 2 min.
Zero plus 20 min. All groups) cease fire.)	
Zero plus 30 min. All groups) open fire.)	Zero plus 30 min. to Zero plus 35 min. 1 belt per min. Zero plus 35 min. to Zero plus 45 min. 1 belt per 2 min.
Zero plus 45 min. All groups) cease fire.)	

5.
(contd) SECOND PHASE.   Rate of Fire.

All guns will open fire at Zero.   Zero to Zero plus 5 min.
                                    1 belt per min. Zero plus
                                    5 min. to Zero plus 25
                                    min. 1 belt per 2 min.
All guns will cease fire at Zero)
    plus 25 min.   )

THIRD PHASE.

   At Zero plus 20 min. Group B 1 will open fire till Zero
plus 25 min. at a rate of 1 belt per min.

6.   In order not to interfere with the present S.O.S. lines,
the 12 guns in reserve (4 guns per Coy.) with teams, will
proceed to the trenches on Zero day in time to take up their
positions by 12 Noon.

   To make up the 12 guns required, O.C. 48th M.G.Coy. will
use L F 4 and 5, L S 3 and 4.

7. Zero day will be notified later
8. Acknowledge

                                    C.J.Wallace
                                         Major.
            General Staff, 16th Division.

SECRET.

47th Machine Gun Coy.
48th Machine Gun Coy.
49th Machine Gun Coy.
"Q" 16th Div.

47th Inf. Bde.)
48th Inf. Bde.) for information.
49th Inf. Bde.)

16th Div. No. D.M.G.O. 151.   13th September, 1917.

Reference 16th Div. No. D.M.G.O. 140 dated 11th September, 1917. Map 57c N.W. Edition 7.A.

1. A Motor lorry will be at 49th M.G. Coys. camp E. MOYENNEVILLE at 8 a.m. 15th September to take teams to the line. Guide to be at road junction leading to camp at 7.45 a.m. 15th September.

2. A Motor lorry will be at ERVILLERS at 8 a.m. 15th September to take 48th and 47th M.G. Coys. teams to the line. Guide from 48th M.G. Coy. to be at Town Majors Office ERVILLERS at 7.45 a.m. 15th September where teams will embus.

3. Route to the line BOYELLES, CRUCIFIX (S.6.d.7.2.) HENIN. Teams will debus at N.33.d.3.9.

4. Os.C. M.G. Coys. will have route from their Camps to debussing point (N.33.d.3.9.) to the line reconnoitred by Officers and drivers, on 14th September.

5. Guns and material will proceed by limber to N.33.d.3.9. in time to arrive there at 9 a.m. 15th September.

6. Weather permitting limbers may proceed to T.4.b.3.5.

7. 2 Motor lorries will be at N.33.d.3.9. at 8 a.m. 16th September to bring teams back to their camps.

Limbers will at that hour be at the same point to bring out the Gun material.

8. All teams will carry one full days rations.

Major,
Machine Gun Officer, 16th Division.

SECRET. Operation Order No 7

Action of M.G. in Minor Operation
(Preliminary)

1. M.Gs of 16th Div. will co-operate with 50th Div. in a minor operation against the enemy's trenches N. of CHERISY. Further details will be issued later.

2. 8 guns of no 2 M.G. Coy will take part. Distribution as follows:—
   2 guns D Sect. under Lt GREAVES
   2 guns B Sect. under Lt WILSON
   4 guns B Sect. under Lt BLUNDELL

3. The above 8 guns will engage enemy trenches N.W. of FONTAINE WOOD.

4. Positions for these guns will be reconnoitred as follows:—
   a) 4 guns D Section, map ref. L.51, L.53, L.54.
   b) 4 guns B Section in HIND TR.

5. Table of targets & rates of fire is attached. Corrections will be supplied by Officers concerned.

6.- The guns are to be in position by 12 noon on Zero Day. Officers concerned will make arrangements for ammunition supply to guns while in action.

7.- All watches will be checked with 151 MG Coy in FARMERS LANE on Zero day at 2 pm.

8.- Zero day & hour will be notified later.

F.A.Milleard. Lt.
A.S.M.G Coy

13-9-17

Attached to OP.7

No. of Shot	Seen from	Target	Range from Being OP	As	Apparent
1	POM ALLEY	Trenches from T6b30 to 0226c500	1300	72°+ 76°	6°48'
2	POM ALLEY	T6c25 to T6c25	1500	80 16	1°35'
3	SHAFT TR	T6a25a85 Village houses from T6a77	1400 to 1450	75° 80°	0°33' 5°1'6" — D Sunken
4	SHAFT TR	U1b.Sh to U6ally Sunk from	1400 to 1440	81°{ 6°42' 61°48'
5	HIND TR	U1c8550 U1b-Sd E0220 E.1	1900	76°	2°52'
6	"	U1b 94 V1b 95 v1	1700	75°	2°11' — B
7	HIND TR. T6 Sh85 T6c 9072	V1a 12	1600	72°	1°56' — Safe
8	HIND TR T6c 05/1	0226 2841	1500	78°	1°41'

Appendix 2
To be attached to
Operation Order No 7.

Minor Operation (Preliminary)

TIME TABLE

1st Phase
Zero to Zero plus 5 — 1 belt per min
Zero plus 5 to Zero plus 20 — 1 belt per 2 min
Zero plus 20 to Zero plus 30 — Cease fire
Zero plus 30 to Zero plus 35 — 1 belt per min
Zero plus 35 to Zero plus 45 — 1 belt per 2 min
Zero plus 45 — Cease fire

2nd Phase
Zero to Zero plus 5 — 1 belt per min
Zero plus 5 to Zero plus 25 — 1 belt per 2 min
Zero plus 25 — Cease fire

3rd Phase
Zero plus 20 to Zero plus 25 — 1 belt per min

Appendix 3

Attach to OO.7.

Ref Timetable (Appendix 2)
about 10,000 rounds will
be required per gun,
i.e. 14 belt boxes
7 boxes SAA
1 petrol tin water.

R. Whitehouse Lt.
45th M. Gy. By.

13-9-7

F.A.41

To O.C. B Section

Ref. O.O.7.—
1 — Guns to be in position and all arrangements completed by noon 15th Sept.
2 — B Section will leave Powerjug Hall at 7:30 am
3 — Zero hour for B phase will be notified at 12 noon 15 Sept in O Section HQ (Sheet 11 3/8)

J.H. Ellis, M Coy — Lt.
for O.C. M Coy.

4-9-7

Ref. No GFG 28

To O.C. 48th M.G. Coy.

Report on Minor Operation
4 p.m. 15/9/17 – 4.30 a.m. 16/9/17.

I was in command of two guns situated respectively at U.1.c. 30.45 & T.6.d. 65.70, targets U.2.b.5.4 to O.32.c.5.1 & U.1.b.5.4 to U.2.a.3.7.

We opened fire at 4 p.m. in accordance with the general plan & for 5 mins. there was no reply. With the exception of those shells which fell on Shaft Trench & in front, the enemy shells went to the rear in the direction of Hind Trench. We ceased fire at 4.20 & resumed at 4.30 p.m. Enemy shortened his range slightly but none fell within 20ˣ of either gun. We ceased fire at 4.45 pm. & shortly after the enemy fire ceased.

Green lights were sent up by the enemy.

The 2nd phase commenced at 7.40pm & the enemy fire was heavier, his HE & shrapnel falling all round. We had no casualties or material damage to guns.

On cease fire at 8.5 pm I mounted my guns in the battle emplacements (which were undamaged) on the S.O.S. line.

At 9 p.m. a large conflagration was observed behind the enemy lines — bearing from LF4 83° true.

There was intermittent enemy shelling during the night & his T.M.'s were active along the Sensée Valley to the right of the new positions.

At 3 a.m. these two guns were again laid on the targets referred to above in anticipation of signals for firing but as it did not appear they were dismounted at 4.30 a.m.

Geo H Weaver 2/Lt
O C D Section

16/9/17

Ref. H.W.2.

Ref. U.T.S. Msg No 202

To O.C. 48 M.G. Coy.

Report on Minor Operation
of September 15/16 1917.

No 1 gun of D Section was stationed
in POM ALLEY at the point
T 6 b 30.65.
No 2 gun was stationed near
POM ALLEY at the point T 6 b 15.85
At 4 p.m. on September 15th
both these guns opened fire on
the enemy trenches N.W. of FON-
TAINE WOOD and in co-operation
with the 50th Division on their left.
The target for No 1 gun was
the point O 32 c 05.05 traversing
to the right to U 2 a 05.25.
For No 2 gun the target was

the point V1 c 8.2 traversing to the left to point V1 c 95.95.

For the first five minutes Fire was opened at the rate of 1 belt per minute and then from 4.5 to 4.20 at the rate of 1 belt per 2 minutes. Cease Fire lasted from 4.20 to 4.30, when fire was opened again till 4.45. The enemy replied with H.E. & shrapnel.

The 2nd Phase began at 7.40 and lasted 25 minutes. For the first 5 minutes fire was maintained at the rate of 1 belt per minute and for the remaining 20 minutes at 1 belt per 2 minutes.

At 4.7 a.m. Sept. 16th the 3rd Phase began and at 4.29 a.m. fire was opened for the next five minutes. This completed the operation.

H. J. Wilson 2/Lt.

Report on Minor Operation
on night 15~16/12/17.

1. "D" Section Guns were
situated in HIND
TRENCH between FAST
LANE and FIT LANE.
Target engaged was
enemy trenches NW of
FONTAINE WOOD.

2. 1st Phase commenced
at 4 pm & finished at
4.45 pm.
At 4.5 pm enemy
Artillery opened fire
mostly using H.E. shell.
Most of the shells fell
in front & behind the
Gun Positions.

3. 2nd Phase commenced
at 7.40 pm & finished

at 8.5 pm.
Enemy sent & handed
sending up two RED
Very Lights & two GREEN.
Enemy Artillery
replied with H.E. Shells.
Most of the Shells fell
in the vicinity of
FIT LANE.
Enemy quiet all the
night.

3. Casualties.-

Scratch on the right
leg by Sgt JENNINGS.
Slight scratch on
the Face. 2/LT. BLUNDELL

4. Ammunition Used.
    33,000 rounds S.A.A.

5. Evacuated position

at 4.45 am 16/9/17.

J H Blundell
2/ Lieut
16/9/17.   O.C. B Section

WAR DIARY

FOR MONTH OF OCTOBER, 1917.

UNIT 48th Machine Gun Coy.

VOLUME NUMBER 19

WAR DIARY
INTELLIGENCE SUMMARY

(Erase heading not required.)

48th M.G. Co.

Army Form C. 2118.

Place	Date	Hour	Summary of Events and Information	Remarks and references to Appendices
CROISILLES	1st Oct	—	Very quiet day. 2 guns from P.O.R. at B.H.Q. fired on Targets laid down by Div. S.O.	
do.	2nd Oct		Conference B.M.G.C.C. at Div HQ.	
do.	3rd Oct		A few shells fell in the vicinity. Enemy aeroplanes flying. A few shells again fell in the vicinity of our Coy HQ at T.17.a.82. 2 guns from CROISILLES fired on targets V.14.B.u.1 and vicinity in conjunction with artillery bombardment at 3 p.m.	
do	4th Oct		"B" Section relieved "A" Section in the C/T Sector. Lieut. F.A. KIRKLAND relieved Capt. D. CAMPBELL at our Coy H.Q. Weather changed to the worse. Very wet weather. Great work and night firing is none.	
do	5th Oct		2 guns co-operated with Stoney T.M. Shoot. Firing was rounds on CTs. Harassing fire at night and usual work.	
do	6th Oct		8 guns co-operated with Div. Arty. Special barrage	

WAR DIARY / INTELLIGENCE SUMMARY

Army Form C. 2118.

Place	Date	Hour	Summary of Events and Information	Remarks and references to Appendices
CROISILLES	6th	6.0	About firing 25 egg rounds. No retaliation. Very wet & foggy. Gun team to 5 pm. A Section from Transport Lines for the shoot.	
do	7th	6.0	Showers, two changes to nozzle bore at 1 gun. Rained all day. Nightly firing as S.M.G.O. programme — 2000 rounds	
do	8th	6.0	Battery licked Co. Hq Hqrs. heavily shelled all day. Down gun B taken back 1400 rounds in equivalent into Artillery. E.A. active in morning.	
do	9th	6.0	Adv. Coy Hq dugout collapsed owing to rain repaired. Work on gun emplacement in CROISILLES. Day quiet.	
do	10th	6.0	Four guns B Section fired 3100 rounds on co-operation with scheduled shoot. Normal shoot at D.M. Conference of M. E. Coy Comdrs at ST. LEGER. S.M. & O. visited guns.	
do	11th	6.0	Capt. D. CAMPBELL relieved Lt. FARRAND in the line. Quiet day.	
do	12th	6.0	Very quiet day, nothing to note.	

Army Form C. 2118.

WAR DIARY
or
INTELLIGENCE SUMMARY
(Erase heading not required.)   48th Machine Gun Co

Instructions regarding War Diaries and Intelligence Summaries are contained in F. S. Regs., Part II. and the Staff Manual respectively. Title Pages will be prepared in manuscript.

Place	Date	Hour	Summary of Events and Information	Remarks and references to Appendices
Morbecque	13th Oct		48th M.G. Co. reconnoitred the ground preparatory to their relieving the Company were right flank.	
do	14th Oct		Relief of whole Company by the 49th M.G. Co. Coy. billeted at Ervillers.	
Ervillers	15th Oct		Cleaning guns and ammunition and making out kit deficiencies. Coy. applied inspection to Divisional M.G. Officer for Gatto Rd.	
do	16th Oct		Guns again stated. Recent experience wanted in respect of petrol.	
do	17th Oct		Coy. practised Infantry drill. Cleaning up Camp.	
do	18th Oct		7.45am Coy paraded for fatigue Bombardier my C.O. Carting Lorries and Ply German prisoners the remains of morning practising position Wilson.	
do	19th Oct		Inspection in full marching order by O.C. Coy. For the remainder of morning lectures and training. Of Section officers.	

Army Form C. 2118.

WAR DIARY
INTELLIGENCE SUMMARY
(Erase heading not required.)

Instructions regarding War Diaries and Intelligence Summaries are contained in F. S. Regs., Part II. and the Staff Manual respectively. Title Pages will be prepared in manuscript.

484 M.G. Co

Place	Date	Hour	Summary of Events and Information	Remarks and references to Appendices
RUYAULCOURT	20th Oct	10 a.m.	Coy parades for fatigues. Inspection by Section Officers. G.O.C. Division inspected	
		2.30 p.m.	the Company in afternoon.	
	21st Oct		Voluntary Church Service. CO and all non commissioned officers reconnoitre the line on right sector of the Divisional front	
ST LEGER	22nd Oct		The Company relieve the 47th M.G.Co in afternoon and took over 16 m.g. positions in the right sector. Coy HQ established at F. 15.c.2.R.	
	23rd Oct		Very quiet day in the line.	
	24th Oct		Another quiet day. The usual night firing was carried out. Work done – general improvement of gun emplacements and dug outs.	
	25th Oct		Repeat of previous day in the line. Ammunition dumps B, C, I.A.A. being replenished. m.g. snipping on RAT ALLEY by day. m.g. intermittent fire on the C.T. kept up by night.	

2449 Wt. W14957/M90 750,000 1/16 J.B.C. & A. Forms/C.2118/12

WAR DIARY
INTELLIGENCE SUMMARY

Army Form C. 2118.

48th M.G.C.

Place	Date	Hour	Summary of Events and Information	Remarks and references to Appendices
ST. LEGER	26th Sept		Very busy day. Preparing Emplacements for Gas attack	
		10pm	at night. In conjunction with Artillery over Iron Barricade	
			7 guns attacked 11,000 rounds were fired in one operation with gas.	
do	27th Oct 3am		10,000 rounds were fired to same area as above.	
	do	3.10pm	In conjunction with Artillery bombardment and T.M.	
		3.35pm	bombarded 4 guns enfilade TURNER TRENCH from	
			JOB to PLUTO; 2 guns enfilade OLDENBURG LANE.	
			All the above guns were fired from GUARDIAN	
			RESERVE. Very little retaliation.	
do	28th W.		Preparing Emplacements for return to work on No 7 M.G. Battery	
			attached to 8th Inf. Byg. For work on Toiskono.	
do	29th W.		48th Inf Bgd. carried out a successful raid on	
			the Eff. at 4.45 pm Three prisoners were captured.	
			11,000 rounds were fired in 30 mins in cooperation	

Army Form C. 2118.

Instructions regarding War Diaries and Intelligence Summaries are contained in F. S. Regs., Part II. and the Staff Manual respectively. Title pages will be prepared in manuscript.

Army Form C. 2118.

WAR DIARY
INTELLIGENCE SUMMARY.
(Erase heading not required.)

48th M.G.C.

Place	Date	Hour	Summary of Events and Information	Remarks and references to Appendices
ST. LEGER	Oct 30th		Day passed quietly. Work continued on new battery position by 87th Coy and RAILWAY RESERVE	
Do	31st Oct		New emplacements dug-out finished at ST. LEGER RESERVE. Enemy shelled S.G. shell hole pits in the vicinity of RAILWAY RESERVE all morning. New barrage positions constructed according to Divisional scheme now almost finished. One section of 87th M.G.C. attached to 48th M.G.C. for the purpose of digging new Emplacements.	

S Hampton Capt
Cmdg 48th Coy M.G.C.

48th Machine Gun Company.

WAR DIARY FOR THE MONTH OF

NOVEMBER 1917

Army Form C. 2118.

WAR DIARY
INTELLIGENCE SUMMARY
(Erase heading not required.)

48th Coy M.G.C.

Place	Date	Hour	Summary of Events and Information	Remarks and references to Appendices
St. LEGER	1st/11/08	—	Company very busy in preparing new forward positions in — (a) RAILWAY RESERVE U.26.c (b) CRUX ROAD V.19.c } Ref. Sheet 57 B S.W. (c) BULL ROAD V.19.d All the material for above positions being drawn from Dump. BUGELET. To large amount of Lag. being carried up. Reserve S.A.A. dumps being formed at each of the above positions. All phones forward of Bde. H.Q. removed.	
	2nd/11/08		Lieut. Sw. Wallace join Coy. H.Q. from Transport Lines. Company engaged in positions in line. During the evening the new front line Battn. & 8 W. York Co. finished their work and Dgn. Coil Company. Entry retaliation heavily in the vicinity KNUCKLE MON & C.	
	3rd/11/08			
	4th/11/08		Two new Emplacements started at head of PELICAN AVENUE. Gave kept up intermittent fire on FAG ALLEY and TRIDENT ALLEY. The north side of THE ALLEY seems to be largely used by the enemy.	
	5th/11/08		Gas attack carried out at night - undergone as in Zoan. Enemy retaliated.	
	6th/11/08		Lt Wade and Men despatched to Bone Depot as surplus officer.	

Army Form C. 2118.

WAR DIARY
or
INTELLIGENCE SUMMARY
(Erase heading not required.)

288 Coy M.G.C.

Instructions regarding War Diaries and Intelligence Summaries are contained in F. S. Regs., Part II. and the Staff Manual respectively. Title Pages will be prepared in manuscript.

Place	Date	Hour	Summary of Events and Information	Remarks and references to Appendices
ST LEGER	6th Nov	Cont	Work being carried on new emplacements (Barrage Positions) 15,000 rds fired during 36 Barrage	
do	7th Nov		Officers of the 288 M.G.Co reconnoitre position in right sector. Preparing for relief.	
ERVILLERS	8th Nov		The Coy is relieved in the morning by 293 M.G.C. and proceed to Rest Camp, ERVILLERS. Baths in ERVILLERS.	
do	9th Nov		Day devoted to cleaning guns + personal equipment.	
do	10th Nov		Guns again thoroughly cleaned. Deficiencies in fm kit + clothing, gas appliances, made out.	
do	11th Nov 10 am		C.of E. Service in CHURCH ARMY hut. Order officer to parade.	
	3.30 pm		R.C's Service in R.E hut.	
	11 am		Presbyterian service in Y.M.C.A hut.	
do	12th Nov		Parades as follows: 7 to 7.45 am Infantry drill under Lt. [?] 9.30 am Inspection by Section Officers 9.30 am do 10 to 10 am Stoppages + Immediate Action taught by Section Officers 11.15 am to 11.15 am Visual training G.O's Conference at Bn HdQrs O.C. Officers + N.C.O's

WAR DIARY or INTELLIGENCE SUMMARY

Army Form C. 2118.

48th Coy. M.C.

Place	Date	Hour	Summary of Events and Information	Remarks and references to Appendices
ERVILLERS	13th Oct		Company Route march in morning. Route as follows :— ERVILLERS — HAMLINCOURT — GOMIECOURT — ERVILLERS. (52)	
ST LEGER	14th Oct		Company suddenly moved for twelve the following morning. The Company formed in morning to relieve the 49th M.G. Co. who is now relieve the 47th M.G. Co. is at the line.	
do	15th Oct		CO. visited trenches in morning. Everybody very quiet.	
do	16th Oct		Preparing maps for an offensive action in the near future. Strong commenced in a large scale on enemy CT's trenches, and new tracks nearby them.	
do	17th Oct		Co. visited trenches and found everything very quiet. Night firing again carried on a large scale.	
do	18th Oct		Very quiet in line. Nothing of importance to note. Day passed quietly. All guns were ready for the attack by the division on the following morning.	
do	19th Oct		Intermittent fire was kept up on enemy tracks and CT's during the night. An Coy. HQ was established at the FACTORY, CROISILLES	

WAR DIARY
or
INTELLIGENCE SUMMARY

Army Form C. 2118.

68th M.G. Co.

Place	Date	Hour	Summary of Events and Information	Remarks and references to Appendices
CROISILLES	20th/XI		At 6.20 a.m. the 16th Divn attacked the Enemy Trenches. TUNNEL TRENCH and TUNNEL SUPPORT captured. The Company find barrage as per 16th Divn "Instructions for an Offensive Action" No. 3.	
do	21st /XI		The enemy attempted a counter attack on the left sector at 6.40 p.m. During this attack Lieut ANDRAIR was killed and Lieut T.H. Blundell wounded; also 4 O.R. all M.G. Casualties were caused by other fire. Enemy attack was repulsed. Copy of Report on the action of 45th Machine Gun Co is attached.	
ST. LEGER	22nd /XI		Coy H.Q. moved back to ST. LEGER. 68th M.G.C. relieved 49th M.G. Co. in the Left Sector and took up its normal war position of that Sector.	
do	23rd/XI		Day passed fairly quietly. At 7 a.m. 47th SB on right made a minor attack. Our Coy were sent up by our troops and a small attack. Our Coy opened fire. 3500 rounds were fired. Our Grounds were very active at night. No firing was done.	

2449 Wt. W14957/M90 750,000 1/16 J.B.C. & A. Forms/C.2118/12

Army Form C. 2118.

WAR DIARY
or
INTELLIGENCE SUMMARY
(Erase heading not required.)

48th M.G. Co.

Place	Date	Hour	Summary of Events and Information	Remarks and references to Appendices
ST LEGER	26/11/16		Tour Teams were found during an enemy artillery bombardment in the morning. One patrol again very active at night. From 7 pm to 8.15 our own heavy guns were lifted to a line East of FONTAINE - BULECOURT ROAD. 2nd Lieut DONALDSON & HARRIES joined Coy. Our patrols again very active at night.	
do	27/11/16		In the Early morning our Gunners finished from runs one enemy L.T.G. & all tracks the patrols my have arrived at might which they reported to be so far no COPSE TRENCH strongly held by the Enemy	
ERVILLERS 28/11/16			The Coy was relieved by 41st M.G. Co. and proceeded to ERVILLERS.	
do	29th NN		2nd Lieut ROCHE 1st Batt Iris. joined the Company from the 10th D.D.B. and remained attached to the Coy until further orders.	

Army Form C. 2118.

WAR DIARY
or
INTELLIGENCE SUMMARY

(Erase heading not required.)

48th M.G. Co.

Instructions regarding War Diaries and Intelligence Summaries are contained in F.S. Regs., Part II. and the Staff Manual respectively. Title Pages will be prepared in manuscript.

Place	Date	Hour	Summary of Events and Information	Remarks and references to Appendices
ERVILLERS	30.9.17		2 Sections orders to proceed up the line at once to strengthen in the defence B, the SENSEE Valley. 2nd Lieut. I.S. McVEY Joined Company from 16th S.D.B. Nothing else to report. 1/10/17	

Humphrey Baker
Capt
O 48th M.G. Co.

5.

Other casualties during this period of heavy shelling were Lieut T.H. Blundell and four other ranks wounded.

After 8 p.m. the situation again became normal.

28/11/17

D'Ampere Capt.
Comdg. 48th M.G. Co.

48th Machine Gun Company.

WAR DIARY FOR THE
MONTH OF
DECEMBER 1917

Army Form C. 2118.

WAR DIARY
or
INTELLIGENCE SUMMARY
(Erase heading not required.)

48th M. G. C.

Place	Date	Hour	Summary of Events and Information	Remarks and references to Appendices
FLETRES	1st Nov		Brigade got short notice to move to ACHIET-LE-PETIT.	
			Coys. marched out at night to rear place with Brigade	
do	2nd Dec		Remaining 2 Coys in line Camp taken over by 121st M.G.Co.	
			½ Coy relieved on trenches by 101st M.G. Coy and moved	
			back to join un-mided Company at ACHIET-LE-PETIT	
			Brigade did not move.	
do	3rd Dec		All was fully Brigade moved to the ROSSIGNOL war	
			moving up at 5 am. Coy in line in BEAVRY.	
do	4th Dec 3:30p		Brigade moved off marching to TAPLEY-13-PO-33E.	
			Then bivouac. E St. EMILIE. Coy left for lines till 11pm	
ST. EMILIE	5th Dec		Coy arrived at St. EMILIE at 6 am. Co. bivouacked the	
			entire day. At night relieved the 153rd Bg. 53rd Div Coy	
			in line, taking up the positions arms of 5 in reserve	
do	6th Dec		C.O. visited line with OC 96th Bde and OC 49th M.G.Co.	
			"C" section relieved by a section from 149th M.G. Coy went	
			back and positions behind RANSOY village	

WAR DIARY or INTELLIGENCE SUMMARY

Army Form C. 2118.

68th M.G.C.

Place	Date	Hour	Summary of Events and Information	Remarks and references to Appendices
ST PAUL I E	7th Dec		Heavy bombardment. No enemy vehicles seen. All our own and enemy M.G.'s quiet. Sent up four new positions to open 6 section HQ at TORBOIS Farm heavily shelled.	
do.	8th Dec		6 section took up new position on X I. Patrols sent out. Loss of an enemy sniper confirmed. All guns not in position for indirect fire achieved. Gas shells and indirect fire.	
do.	9th Dec		At BUSH ETTES wood. 2 guns D section were put in position on ridge 47" — 96, and at FORT RD. Good observation obtained. M.G. position started on rides.	
do.	10th Dec		Work continued in new bivouacs and running into Lieut Ers Wallace went on leave. CO visited the transport lines.	
do.	11th Dec		Very frosty. Difficulty being experienced into gun emplacements owing to frozen earth. Artillery active.	

Army Form C. 2118.

WAR DIARY
or
INTELLIGENCE SUMMARY.
(Erase heading not required.)

45th M.G.Co.

Place	Date	Hour	Summary of Events and Information	Remarks and references to Appendices
S. EMILIE	12th Dec		Harassing fire kept up throughout the night on enemy roads. This work was done by 2 guns at BASSE-BOULOGNE	
do	13th Dec		Heavy bombardment in the morning on our left. All M.G.'s "stood to". Third Land Front	
do	14th Dec		Slight alteration in dispositions of guns. New positions are being made are being made	
do	15th Dec		Set the batteries [?] [?] [?] [?] [?] hand harassing fire during night. 300 rounds a fired. Heavy firing on our left at night. Much sickness in the Company owing to bad accommodation on line and the rough weather. 2 guns "C" Subsection relieved 2 guns at 7th H.L.I. SUBSECTION HQ.	
do	16th Dec		Alteration in position. All guns remain same sight. Fine winter weather. Every shelter [?] shelters.	
do	17th Dec		Some [?] [?] [?] expedient. Work on RAPTORS POST held up on account of heavy shelling	
do	18th Dec		Very quiet day on the line. Work on G repair.	

Army Form C. 2118.

WAR DIARY
INTELLIGENCE SUMMARY.
(Erase heading not required.)

45th M.G.C.

Place	Date	Hour	Summary of Events and Information	Remarks and references to Appendices
ST EMILIE	19th Dec		Employed began by C Section around very hard tho much better in the line	
do	20th Dec		Enemy aeroplanes very busy daily for the past week or so. This gun specially trained as A.A. mounting to deal with E.A.	
do	21st Dec		Foggy weather chiefly. Enemy quiet in line. Nothing of interest to note. Our guns the reserve answer of any night on enemy roads and tracks.	
do	22nd Dec		Went to warm bath and Expenses by A. Sutton	
do	20th Dec		BRAY - BOULOGNE flight shelled during night otherwise fair	
do	23rd Dec		ST EMILIE very heavy shelled between 7.30pm & 12pm very quiet day little firing done by ourselves or Enemy	
do	24th Dec		Relief of 69th M.G.C. Company in line in the afternoon. Another quiet day.	
do	25th Dec		Cos relieved after a period of 22 days in line with 16 guns out of 96.	

Army Form C. 2118.

WAR DIARY
INTELLIGENCE SUMMARY.

48th M.G.C.

(Erase heading not required.)

Place	Date	Hour	Summary of Events and Information	Remarks and references to Appendices
TINCOURT	28th Dec.		Cleaning Guns. Billets for Off. & men good. Billets & accommodation for Transport fair, whole Coy at Centre at night.	
"	29th Dec		Making out lists of deficiencies. Moved room. 48th Inf Bde relieved in line & also relieved in TINCOURT.	
"	30th Dec		Company Dinner.	
"	31st Dec		Parades for cleaning guns. majority of Coy on fatigues	

D Campbell Capt.
O.C. 48th M.G.C.

48th COMPANY,
MACHINE GUN
CORPS.
No.
Date 31/12/17.

WAR DIARY,

FOR MONTH OF JANUARY, 1918.

VOLUME: 22

UNIT: 118th Machine Gun Coy. M.G.C.

Army Form C. 2118.

WAR DIARY
INTELLIGENCE SUMMARY. 48th M.G.C.
(Erase heading not required.)

Place	Date	Hour	Summary of Events and Information	Remarks and references to Appendices
TINCOURT	Jan 1st		Officers reconnoitre left sector preparatory to relief. Capt Campbell went on leave.	
do	Jan 2nd		Preparation for going into the line. Parties by buses from HAMEL & Ste EMILIE and others 47 in Coy. in the left section. HQ Ste EMILIE. Relief completed 6.30pm	
Ste EMILIE	Jan 3rd		Left hand hand went during early morning. MATASSISE FARM shelled.	
do	Jan 4th		Usual night firing. 2000 rounds on F.A. MATASSISE FARM shelled.	
do	Jan 5th		4000 rounds night firing. Ste EMILIE, Railway Embankment and MATASSISE FARM shelled at night.	
do	Jan 6th		Still freezing. E.A. dropt bombs in early morning on work areas. EPEHY hard shelled. Major BLACKER's = M.C. in London Gazette. Usual night firing.	
do	Jan 7th		Bde HQ shelled this morning and afternoon. Vicinity of Railway Embankment and EPEHY shelled	

Army Form C. 2118.

WAR DIARY
INTELLIGENCE SUMMARY.

(Erase heading not required.)

48th M.G.Co

Place	Date	Hour	Summary of Events and Information	Remarks and references to Appendices
SKEMILIE	8.1.18		Guns No 17,18,19 relieved by 49 M.G.Coy and new positions taken up. Four barrage and numbering scheme came into force. D section HQ moved to RAILWAY EMBANKMENT. Work on tunnel through embankment continued. D HQ enlarged. F.14 shelled intermittently.	S.D.26 attached
do	9.1.17		Test S.O.S. sent up at at 4.30 and 9.30pm. Guns could not see it. MARASSIE FARM shelled during the day. All our camps could be seen for guns.	
do	10.1.17	9.30pm	A heavy bombardment with shell fire on left of Divisional front but nothing followed. Carried on with duties. Normal night firing.	
do	11.1.17		Another bombardment on the left this morning at 5 and 6 again not affecting the Divisional front. ENEMY - SKEMILIE had shells from 6.3 inch.	
		10.30pm	Left section HQ shelled. Normal night firing. Work in progress on new emplacements.	

WAR DIARY
INTELLIGENCE SUMMARY
23rd July

Army Form C. 2118.

Place	Date	Hour	Summary of Events and Information	Remarks and references to Appendices
SENLIS	12.7.18		Still in TETARD WOOD. Enemy Gun fire barrage fire started at 3.30pm, shooting for front of Regt return HQ.	
	13.7.18		S/Lts ? Enquired minor dispatch infants by M.I. Travelling log. All aircraft very active. At 10 am our 8 our planes attacked 2 S.E. enemy one shown behind his own lines and bringing the other down in flames went SART FARM. During the afternoon one of our planes was forced to land near MAURBISE FARM at 4.30pm. 15A fired on our lines and fired one of own billows. its own autiguouts shot down by M.M. fire. 2250 rounds were fired at F.A. during the day. Small lived shells.	
do	14.7.18		Day very quiet. Own aircraft active. Night firing as usual. EAGLE BATTRY reported 2500 rounds.	

Army Form C. 2118.

WAR DIARY
INTELLIGENCE SUMMARY.
(Erase heading not required.)

45th M.G.C.

Place	Date	Hour	Summary of Events and Information	Remarks and references to Appendices
SKEMLIK	15	1.18	Enemy activity very active in front of ENEMY RAGIL DUARRY fired on again at night. Work greatly hindered by those conditions. Artillery very bad and troops required everywhere.	
do	16.1.18		Intermittent shelling by Fld artillery. Nothing else of importance happened.	
do	7.1.18		6 Tank teams enemy raided HAYTROP POST under cover of a bombardment. N.C.O. went up. Six guns fired on SOS line at slow rate. Two Officers attached from RDF. Ferry Shells near Coy HQ SKEMLIE at 6.45 p.m. Enemy Artillery bombarded KILDARE POST and HOLD BANK during the day. Road arrivals fired on twice tonight by MGs during the night.	
do	16	1.18	A section guns and HQ also D section HQ shelled. Enemy aircraft active. Night firing on KILDARE BANK and	

Army Form C. 2118.

WAR DIARY
INTELLIGENCE SUMMARY.
(Erase heading not required.)

48th M.G. Co.

Place	Date	Hour	Summary of Events and Information	Remarks and references to Appendices
Sh.EMILIE.	16.1.18		HOLTS BANK.	
do.	19.1.18		Six EMILIE shelled. Usual work and night-firing	
do.	20.1.18		Six EMILIE and batteries in vicinity shelled. Company relieved by 49th M.G. Coy and moves to TINCOURT. Divisional M.G. Coy. arrives.	TINCOURT OO.27 (attached)
TINCOURT	21.1.18		Cleaning guns, equipment, baths &c.	
do	22.1.18		Section Training under Section Officers. Lieut E.I.W. WALLACE to U.K. on substitute.	
do	23.1.18		A + B Sections go up to Six EMILIE to work on reserve positions. b.O.R. Brigade visits billets. Lecture for C and D sections.	
do	24.1.18		C + D sections carry on with work at reserve positions. Reminder if Company expected by Divisional Commander.	
do	25.1.18		Inspection by Corps Commander expected but did not materialise. General cleaning up of billets and vicinity &c.	

Army Form C. 2118.

WAR DIARY
INTELLIGENCE SUMMARY
(Erase heading not required.)

48th M.G.C.

Instructions regarding War Diaries and Intelligence Summaries are contained in F.S. Regs., Part II. and the Staff Manual respectively. Title pages will be prepared in manuscript.

Place	Date	Hour	Summary of Events and Information	Remarks and references to Appendices
INCOURT	27-1-18		Company inspected by S.O. 48 Brigade. 2.W.'s NCO's in a course for care of pigeons.	
	28-1-18		Company Church Parade. Subsequently rest for the remainder of the day.	
	29-1-18		Company training. — Lectures gun work, revolvers and gas drill. Capt Campbell returning from leave. t.A action at night but no bombs near.	
	30-1-18		Company preparing for the line, cleaning guns, packing limbers etc in morning, afternoon Coy paraded by rail to the line and relieves 49th M.G.C.	
ST EMILIE	31-1-18		A large amount of work in hand in the line. Very misty day and everything very quiet in the line.	

D Humphris Capt
O.C. 48th M.G.Co.

48th COMPANY,
MACHINE GUN
31/1/18

SECRET   48 Company M.G.C.
           Operation Order N° 26

1. On night 8/9 January, the following alterations will take place.

2. O.C. "C" Section will arrange to take over M.G. N° 20 from O.C. B Section.

3. Three guns of "B" Section at M.G. N°s 17, 18 and 19 will be relieved by 49 M.G. Coy at about 5·30 P.M.

4. Everything, including "N° boards and order boards" will be taken out except S.A.A. trench and aerial mountings "T" pieces, foolproofs and range charts

5. These three teams on relief will proceed to Section HQ BASSE BOULOGNE where they will meet and load limbers as follows:—   1 team ____ ½ limber
                     2 teams ____ 1 limber.

6. They will then proceed to B Section HQ where they will meet guides.

7. O.C. "C" Section will detail one guide for new position at M.G. 24. O.C. D Section will detail two guides for M.G. 28 and new position at M.G. 29. Guides to be at "B" HQ at 6 P.M.

8. The team of "B" for M.G. 24 will proceed to position and come under O.C. "C" Section

9. O.C. "B" and remaining two teams of "B" will proceed as follows:— 1 team will relieve team of "A" Section at M.G. 28. 1 team will occupy new position at M.G. 29. O.C. "B" will make his HQ with O.C. "D"

10. Team of A Section when relieved, will load on limber and proceed to A.HQ when it will come under O.C. "A" and occupy new N° M.G. 27.

11. O.C. "C" will arrange to inter-change teams of "C" at MG24 and "B" at 20 during the night. Both positions at 24 will then come under 2nd Lt. M°VEY. O.C "C" will be responsible for his own Section only.

12. A revised BARRAGE and system of numbering will be issued later

13. Acknowledge
8·1·18

F.A.Hickels LT
48 M.G.CoY

48 Company M.G.C.
Operation Order No 27

1. The 48 M.G. Coy will be relieved by the 49 M.G. Coy in the LEFT SECTOR on the 20TH JANUARY 1917.

2. Guides for Section HQ will be at Coy HQ at 2.30 PM.

3. Section officers will arrange for guides for gun teams to be at their Section HQ.

4. The following will be handed over and receipts obtained. Tripods. Belt Boxes. Range cards. Gum boots. Order boards and telephones.

5. Petrol tins will be brought out.

6. Limbers will arrive at Section HQrs one hour after relieving sections.

7. Limbers will be required as follows.
   C and ½ B --- 1 Limber   D and ½ B -- 1 Limber.
   A -------- 1 Limber

8. On relief, company will assemble at ST EMELIE and entrain for TINCOURT.

9. LT. NR. LEE. will proceed to TINCOURT on the morning of the 20TH and take over billets from 49 M.G. Coy

10. Transport and QM Stores will move under own arrangements

11. Acknowledge.

E.W. Wallace.
LT
48 Company M.G.C.

19.1.18

48 Coy. M.G.C.

OPERATION ORDER N⁰ 28

1. The 48th M.G.C. will relieve the 49th M.G.C. in the left sector to-morrow the 30th inst.

2. The Coy (less Transport) will parade at Coy. H.Q. at 1.45 p.m, and move off at 2.0 p.m.

3. T.O. will take over 49th M.G.Coy. Transport Lines at VILLERS FAUCON. He will make his own arrangements for the move. Gun limbers & H.Q. limbers must be at ST EMILIE by 3.30 p.m.
   Guides will meet Coy at ST. EMILIE H.Q at 3.30 p.m.

4. Rations will be drawn at ST. EMILIE

5. The following are the dispositions of the Sections:-

A Section	Positions	21. 22. 27. 28
B do.	do.	23. 24. 25. 26
C do.	do.	29. 30. 31. 32
D do.	do.	17. 18. 19. 20

6. All attached men at present in A, B & D Sections will be attached to C Section as from to-morrow.

7. All Trench Stores with the exception of Petrol Tins will be taken over. Telephones are to be handed over

8. Relief complete will be notified to Coy. H.Q

   J.A. Middleton 2/Lt.
   48 Coy. M.G.C.

29. 1. 1918

WAR DIARY.

FOR MONTH OF FEBRUARY, 1918.

VOLUME:- 23

UNIT:- 48th Machine Gun Company

48th Machine Gun Company.

WAR DIARY FOR THE

MONTH OF

FEBRUARY 1918.

Army Form C. 2118.

WAR DIARY
OF
INTELLIGENCE SUMMARY.

(Erase heading not required.)

48th M.G.C.

Place	Date	Hour	Summary of Events and Information	Remarks and references to Appendices
Field	1st Feb.		Three new emplacements started in L/Cpl Britton's also reconnaissance for same. Harassing fire was kept up at the enemy at SAPOS LOOP, MOTTS BANK & KILDARE POST.	
"	2nd Feb		2000 rds. were fired on EAGLE QUARRY, KILDARE POST now MOTTS BANK.	
"	3rd Feb		Quiet day. Usual harassing fire kept up at night.	
"	4th Feb		At 10.30 p.m. L.O.S. Signal was sent up & rapid rate gun fire opened out at a slow rate of fire.	
"	5th Feb		Heavy bombardment in morning. Brigade reserve line.	
"	6th Feb		Relieved by 47th M.G.C. and proceeded to VILLERS FAUCON.	
VILLERS FAUCON	7th Feb		Lieut. A. KIRKLAND M.C., L/Cpl NICKSON M.M., Cpl SNELLING M.M., Pte KEARNEY M.M. presented with medal ribands at HAMEL hut by G.O.C. IV Army.	
"	8th Feb		All fighting limber packed and carefully inspected by C.O. Also personal equipment of men.	

Army Form C. 2118.

WAR DIARY
INTELLIGENCE SUMMARY
(Erase heading not required.)

48th - M.G.C.

Place	Date	Hour	Summary of Events and Information	Remarks and references to Appendices
Field	9th Sept		Parade as follows - Lecture by Section Officers. Phys Tr - Musketry	
(Villers-Faucon)	10th		2nd Lieut J.B. Service attached to DM.G.O's office. Church Parade. Coy Plays Inter Section Team as follows.	
	11th		cm Sect. 3-1. 2nd Lieut Greener leaves for P.I. Course at 17. Div. Lieut G.B. Green joins Coy as 2nd i/c. Company	
	12th Sept		engaged in trotting shields, anti-walls, 3' high, around huts. Coy talked to Divisional Theatre, HAMEL by Brig.	
"	13th		Grady - Revolver Practice - Mechanism, Coy engaged on some "fatigue" as previous days.	
	14th			
	15th			
St Emilie	15th			
	16th		Quiet day	
	17th			
	18th			

WAR DIARY
or
INTELLIGENCE SUMMARY

Army Form C. 2118.

ASE/A.G.C.O

(Erase heading not required.)

Place	Date	Hour	Summary of Events and Information	Remarks and references to Appendices
Hill 10	R6		B11 Co went to HQ Co to continue training & other duties	
	20		Went to [illegible] of situation & conditions	
			West Line continued. R3 material sent to R10 dump opposite	
	21		14th Sept 1.47 BM 4 No activity	
		4.45 AM	Heavy [illegible] it drove in. Our posts took him lot A? As 28 opened SOS [illegible] heavy shell fire attention and time. UN tanks out [illegible] off shelter during at 5.30 shells feel 25000 rds & [illegible]	
			N Co a section on duty up [illegible] 700 rds hut shelter IF Company suit BM6C & OC Comp In sheds [illegible]	
	22		Down from 269 Co 9am to 9pm. Drew from 97 refill for work shelters to deepen & thin shafts at R3, R1916 + R10 dump for Cawdor & mr Dunily Co. New trenches at R7, R8, R5, R6 + R10 commenced. Also shelters at R8, R6, R17 & R10.	

Army Form C. 2118.

WAR DIARY
or
INTELLIGENCE SUMMARY
(Erase heading not required.)

Instructions regarding War Diaries and Intelligence Summaries are contained in F. S. Regs., Part II. and the Staff Manual respectively. Title Pages will be prepared in manuscript.

AQ 5 M.G.C.

Place	Date	Hour	Summary of Events and Information	Remarks and references to Appendices
Field	23rd		Work on new positions shelters. Increased with No firing. Hostile shelling. Work as per attached.	
"	24th		E.A. fired at Guns flashes of enemy artillery spotted & on whites informed at up 157.158. Sounded series positions. Shelter for R.S. Constructed. Work as per attached.	
"	25th		M.G. team spotted near Villers Guislain Sap to hostile hilltop informed. Work on hostile shelters & dugouts as per attached.	
"	26th		S.A. fired at. War crater attacked.	
"	27th		Raid on left. Supported by 2 guns. Fired 4000 rds. Relieved by Officers noted time.	
"	28th		Artillery activity by enemy beyond Adons in Trees increased. S.O.S. 500 rds at S.A. S.A. action. Work as usual. Fired on S.O.S. lines.	

Signed /s/

48th COMPANY,
MACHINE GUN
CORPS.

No............
Date............

48 Coy. M.G.C.   Copy No. 16
                                         5-2-18.
Operation order No. 29

I. The 48th M.G.Coy will be relieved by the 47th M.G.Coy on the evening of 6th inst

II. On relief the Coy will proceed to billets at VILLERS-FAUCON

III. Guides for Section H.Q. will be at Coy H.Q ST. EMILIE at 4.30 p.m

IV. All Trench Stores will be handed over, also A.A. Sights, one Petrol tin per gun team and one per Section H.Q.

V. Limbers will be required as follows:—
   1 Limber - D section H.Q at 6.30 p.m.
   1 Limber - ½A   do (M.G. Service)   do   do.
   1 Limber - B   do   H.Q   do   do.
   2 Limbers - C   do   H.Q   do   do.

VI. O.C. "C" Section will arrange to have party working on mined dug-out till 8.0 p.m when they will be relieved by a party of 47th M.G. Coy

ACKNOWLEDGE

                                J. A. Kinnear, LIEUT.
                                48 Coy. M.G.C.

Issued at 8.0 pm.

SECRET

48th COMPANY,
MACHINE GUN
CORPS.

Copy N° 9
Date 14-2-18

Operation Order N° 28
By
LT. C.C. GREEN commanding 48 M.G.Coy.

1. The 48 M.G.Coy will relieve 110 M.G.Coy in the EPÉHY Sector on the 15th February.

2. Guns of 110 M.G.Coy are divided as follows:—
   N° 1 Group ———————— R4 R5 R6 R7 R8 and R9
   N° 2 "   ———————— R10 R11 R12 R13 and R14
   N° 3 "   ———————— R1 R2 R3 R15 and R16

3. Sections will take over positions as follows:—
   N° 1 Group —— "A" Section (4 Guns) plus Sub-Section of "C"
       A — N° R5 R6 R7 and R8   "C" R4 and R9

   N° 2 Group —— B Section (4 guns) plus 1 team of "C"
       B Section R11 R12 R13 R14. "C" Section R10

   N° 3 Group —— D Section (4 guns) and 1 team of "C" Section
       D Section R1 R2 R15 R16   "C" Section R3

4. Groups will be commanded by
   N° 1 Group ———— 2nd LT. H.F. WILSON.
   N° 2   "   ———— 2nd LT. J. DONALDSON.
   N° 3   "   ———— 2nd LT. B.A. HARRIES.

   2nd LT. J.S. McVEY will command "C" Sub-Section of group I.
   2nd LT. G.E.L. RICHARDSON will be attached to group 2.

5. GUIDES will be provided as follows:—
   N° 1 group South end of HIGH ST EPÉHY at 12 NOON.
   R7 and R8 teams will wait at battle HQ until 6-30 pm, when they will go up with guides and limbers of 110 M.G.Coy to positions.
   N° 2 group at MORGAN POST, at junction of roads N end of HIGH ST at 11-30 am. There will be guides for each gun team and one for Section Officers.
   N° 3 group guide for R1, R2, R3 and Section Officer on EPÉHY — ST EMELIE RD, 100x S of EPÉHY at 12-15 PM.
   Guide for R15 and R16 on SAULCOURT—EPÉHY 300x W of EPÉHY at 11-30 am.

2

6. **Limbers** are required as follows:-
   No. 1 group --- 2   No. 3 group --- 2
   No. 2   "   --- 2   HQ --- 2 and Mess Cart

7. **Time of leaving** VILLIERS FAUCON will be
   HQ --- 10.30 am.   No. 1 group --- 11 am
   No. 2 group --- 10.30 am.   No. 3 group --- { R1, R2, R3 --- 11.15 am
                                                { R15, R16 --- 10.30 am

   (A) R15 and R16 will accompany Group 2 to HIGH ST EPEHY when they will branch off on SAULCOURT RD to positions.

8. All ammunition, trench stores, **maps, range cards** etc will be taken over and receipts given. Copies to be sent to battle HQ (except for R7 and R8) by 6 PM. All guns, tripods and B.boxes will be taken in

9. O.C Sections will take over present S.O.S lines and battle lines and firing programme as used by 110 MG Coy, and will ensure that all teams understand them

10. Company BATTLE HQ will be at RAILWAY EMBANKMENT, F.I.b.70.05, by 2 PM. Section officers will find out Battalion HQ for their Sector and must report to them daily.
    Company HQ will be at ST EMILIE.

11. The ration dump will be at the church, EPÉHY. F.I.c.8.9. Each gun team will send ration party to be at dump at 4 PM on 15TH inst, and 3 PM on subsequent days. Water will be drawn in EPEHY village by ration parties.

12. Relief complete will be **reported** to battle HQ by runner

13. Acknowledge

    Copies to
    1... D.M.G.C.   8... T.O.
    2... O.C 48 M.G.Coy   9.10. War diary
    3... 49 Inf Bde
    4-7... O.C Sections

F. N. Undsea Jr
48th M. G. Coy.

TABLE "B"

ENTRAINING STATION. ----------------------------------ESQUELBECQ.

Date.	Time of departure.	Unit.	Time of arrival.	
			Time.	Date.
21st.	1.20p.m.	7th. R.Irish Rifles. 1 Coy., 10th. R.Dublin Fus,	9.20p.m.	21st.
21st.	5.20p.m.	145th. Coy. A.S.C. 155th. Field Coy. R.E.	1.20.am.	22nd.
21st.	9.20p.m.	Headquarters, 48th. Inf. Bde. 48th. Inf. Bde. Sig. Section. 48th. M.G. Coy. 48th. T.M.Bty.	5.20a.m.	22nd.
22nd.	1.20a.m.	2nd. R. Dublin Fusiliers. 1 Coy., 10th. R.Dublin Fus.	9.20a.m.	22nd.
22nd.	5.20a.m.	8th. R. Dublin Fusiliers. 1 Coy., 10th. R.Dublin Fus.	1.20p.m.	22nd.
22nd.	9.20a.m. *JnB*	9th. R. Dublin Fusiliers. 1 Coy., 10th. R.Dublin Fus. *H Qr 10 R Dub Fus*	5.20p.m.	22nd.
22nd.	1.20p.m.	11th. Hants (P) (less 1 Coy)	9.20p.m.	22nd.
22nd.	5.20p.m.	112th. Field Ambulance.	1.20a.m.	23rd.

DISTRIBUTION OF 16TH. DIVISION ADMN. ORDER 31.

Copy No.		No. of copies.
1.	G.O.C.	1.
2.	"G" Branch.	1.
3.	16th. Div. Engrs.	4.
4.	47th. Inf. Brigade.	7.
5.	48th. Inf. Brigade.	7.
6.	49th. Inf. Brigade.	7.
7.	11th. Hants (P).	1.
8.	16th. Div. Signal Co.R.E.	1.
9.	16th. Div. Train.	5.
10.	S.S.O., 16th. Div.	1.
11.	A.D.M.S.	4.
12.	D.A.D.V.S.	2.
13.	D.A.D.O.S.	1.
14.	A.P.M.	1.
15.	Camp Commandant.	2.
16.	No. 4 D.S.C.	1.
17.	Traffic, Hazebrouck.	1.
18.	Postal Service.	1.

www.ingramcontent.com/pod-product-compliance
Lightning Source LLC
Chambersburg PA
CBHW080858230426
43663CB00013B/2569